# MORMON
## *Mighty Man of God*

# Mormon
## Mighty Man of God

### Angus H. Belliston

CFI
Springville, Utah

ISBN 13:978-1-559955-132-6

Published by CFI, an imprint of Cedar Fort, Inc., 2373 W. 700 S., Springville, UT, 84663
Distributed by Cedar Fort, Inc. www.cedarfort.com

LIBRARY OF CONGRESS CATALOGING-IN-PUBLICATION DATA

Belliston, Angus H.
  Mormon, mighty man of God / Angus H. Belliston.
    p. cm.
  ISBN 978-1-59955-132-6
  1. Mormon (Book of Mormon figure)  I. Title.

  BX8627.4.M67B45 2007
  289.3'22—dc22

2007046981

Cover design by Jeremy Beal
Cover design © 2008 by Lyle Mortimer
Edited and typeset by Lyndsee Simpson Cordes

Printed in the United States of America

10  9  8  7  6  5  4  3  2  1

Printed on acid-free paper

This book is dedicated to my children and grandchildren, whose faith in the teachings of the Book of Mormon will lead them to righteousness, happiness, and prosperity.

# ACKNOWLEDGMENTS

I would like to gratefully acknowledge the encouragement of my wife, Jenny, and the expert assistance of my children, especially the hours of editorial and composition help by Janine, Anne, and James.

# CONTENTS

# INTRODUCTION

Mormon—mighty Mormon—has yet to be fully discovered! In studying the Book of Mormon, I have been increasingly impressed with the awesome stature of its principal writer—the great prophet Mormon. Serious reflection will bring to mind his three amazing careers, all of which he pursued at the same time: 1) commander of armies, 2) writer of history, and 3) the Lord's prophet. As we read with this in mind, it becomes apparent that this man is unique in the history of this world.

I decided to put down my thoughts about Mormon, mostly for my own satisfaction and for my family and friends. I'm pleased that others have enjoyed it too. This is my testimony of a man whom I regard as one of the great human beings of all time.

In all the world's history, there has never been a commander of armies who led his troops for as long as seventy-five years, let alone one who survived so long through a continuing war of extermination.

I don't know of any writer in all the world's history who has been so prolific in his achievement and so unique in the kind of history he wrote.

Prophets often experience limited results during their own time, and Mormon was no exception. But his purpose was clear: many hundreds of years after his death, the Book of Mormon was brought to light and it changed the world.

If one were to find a man matching any of these achievements, how likely would it be to find one man matching all three? Yet Mormon was such a man.

One of the great characters of all ages, Mormon is still largely unknown to many. Millions of people all around the world are known as Mormons. But even many members of the Church may not know their namesake well, or fully appreciate this lonely giant of history. This amazing human being, who has so profoundly impacted our world and our culture, deserves our closer attention.

The dimensions of Mormon's work were largely unknown in his own time and among his own people. Fifteen hundred years after his death, the world that had never known him heard of his life and times through the Book of Mormon.

Mormon is a writer of unusual ability. The clarity and power of his expression bring his writing to life. His own words cannot be improved upon. I hope that the reader of this little volume will enjoy the extensive use of quotations from Mormon's great book. As you read again these famous passages, please consider them as a guided tour into the life and teachings of this man. You will learn more about him, about his heroic contributions to mankind, and about the book that is changing the world.

Like a few others who lived in the obscurity of the distant past, Mormon's legacy is prodigious. He should be discovered by us all!

PART ONE

# *Mormon*
## THE MAN

*chapter one*
# THE LIFE OF MORMON

Mormon was a magnificent man. He was at once a mighty warrior, a historian without peer, and a prophet of the Lord. My purpose here is not to write a biography; we really don't know that much about him. Instead I will give the reader a short sketch of the man, his work, and his teachings.

Although the details are unclear, we know more about this man than about many of the other prominent personalities in the scriptures. He was born about 1700 years ago, in the year AD 311, somewhere in the ancient Americas. He was a pure descendant of Father Lehi, and he was the son of another Mormon (see 3 Nephi 5:20; Mormon 1:5). He was taught in person by the Savior, whom he saw in a vision when he was fifteen, and he was later ministered to by the Three Nephites (see Mormon 1:15; 8:11). He described in considerable detail the political and social circumstances of his time and fully expressed both his thoughts and his personal feelings. His greatest hope—for the recovery of his people from their journey to destruction—was frustrated. His greatest joy was in his knowledge of the Savior. His constant prayer was for us of the latter days.

While he may not yet have been fully appreciated, Mormon has not been ignored. One of the world's greatest books bears his name. The world's only true religion is better known by his name than by its real name. He is regularly featured in pageants and sermons. But considering the contribution he made during his long life and his uniqueness among great men, he is worthy of additional attention.

Perhaps he has been unintentionally upstaged by his famous son. Moroni, in many ways, has stolen the show. It was he who drew the long-awaited assignment to bring back to earth the gospel of Jesus Christ. He was the "mighty angel flying" in fulfillment of revelation. His appearance to Joseph Smith and the delivery of the sacred record won Moroni a place on the spires of most of the LDS temples in the world. Moroni deserves all the attention he has received. He was the single, gallant, lonely survivor of all the Nephite battles. He endured to the end with a faithfulness unsurpassed.

It is Moroni who provides us, on the title page, with our introduction to the Book of Mormon.[1] As Moroni wrote about the coming forth of this sacred volume, he was speaking of the life's work of his father. Let us begin our study of Mormon by reading Moroni's introduction:

> Wherefore, [the Book of Mormon] is an abridgment of the record of the people of Nephi, and also of the Lamanites—Written to the Lamanites, who are a remnant of the house of Israel; and also to Jew and Gentile—Written by way of commandment, and also by the spirit of prophecy and of revelation—Written and sealed up, and hid up unto the Lord . . . To come forth by the gift and power of God unto the interpretation thereof—Sealed by the hand of Moroni, and hid up unto the Lord, to come forth in due time by way of the Gentile—The interpretation thereof by the gift of God.
>
> An abridgment taken from the Book of Ether also, which is a record of the people of Jared . . . Which is to show unto the remnant of the House of Israel what great things the Lord hath done for their fathers; and that they may know the covenants of the Lord, that they are not cast off forever—And also to the convincing of the Jew and Gentile that Jesus is the Christ, the eternal God. (Title page of the Book of Mormon)

This is Moroni's testimony of the gospel his father so cherished and taught to him:

> [The Book of Mormon] shall be brought out of darkness unto light, according to the word of God; yea, it shall be brought out of the earth, and it shall shine forth out of darkness, and come unto the knowledge of the people; and it shall be done by the power of God. . . .
>
> For the eternal purposes of the Lord shall roll on, until all his

promises shall be fulfilled. . . .

And no one need say they shall not come, for they surely shall, for the Lord hath spoken it; for out of the earth shall they come, by the hand of the Lord, and none can stay it; and it shall come in a day when it shall be said that miracles are done away; and it shall come even as if one should speak from the dead.

And it shall come in a day when the blood of saints shall cry unto the Lord, because of secret combinations and the works of darkness.

Yea, it shall come in a day when the power of God shall be denied, and churches become defiled and be lifted up in the pride of their hearts; yea, even in a day when leaders of churches and teachers shall rise in the pride of their hearts, even to the envying of them who belong to their churches.

Yea, it shall come in a day when there shall be heard of fires, and tempests, and vapors of smoke in foreign lands;

And there shall also be heard of wars, rumors of wars, and earthquakes in divers places.

Yea, it shall come in a day when there shall be great pollutions upon the face of the earth; there shall be murders, and robbing, and lying, and deceivings, and whoredoms, and all manner of abominations; when there shall be many who will say, Do this, or do that, and it mattereth not, for the Lord will uphold such at the last day. But wo unto such, for they are in the gall of bitterness and in the bonds of iniquity.

Yea, it shall come in a day when there shall be churches built up that shall say: Come unto me, and for your money you shall be forgiven of your sins. . . .

Behold, I speak unto you as if ye were present, and yet ye are not. But behold, Jesus Christ hath shown you unto me, and I know your doing.

And I know that ye do walk in the pride of your hearts; and there are none save a few only who do not lift themselves up in the pride of their hearts, unto the wearing of very fine apparel, unto envying, and strifes, and malice, and persecutions, and all manner of iniquities; and your churches, yea, even every one, have become polluted because of the pride of your hearts.

For behold, ye do love money, and your substance, and your fine apparel, and the adorning of your churches, more than ye love the poor and the needy, the sick and the afflicted. (Mormon 8:16, 22, 26–32, 35–37)

In all the world's history, there has not been another life to match that of Mormon, the mighty man of God. There are none like him. In all the world, there is not a book with a message so unique as that of the book written by this man.

Mormon's message in the Book of Mormon is another testament of the greatest man of all, the Savior Jesus Christ. Of the Savior, an unintended tribute was once spoken by the infamous Pontius Pilate: "Behold the man!" (John 19:5). Of Mormon, who testified so remarkably of the Savior, we are moved with earnest admiration to exclaim likewise—Behold the man!

Notes
1. Joseph Smith, *History of the Church of Jesus Christ of Latter-day Saints*, ed. B. H. Roberts (Salt Lake City: The Church of Jesus Christ of Latter-day Saints, 1932–51), 1:71.

*chapter two*

# THE MIGHTY WARRIOR

Mormon began as a military man. His career as a soldier spanned at least sixty years, probably more. During his lifetime, he was immersed in one of the world's most devastating wars of annihilation. Never in his life was there a period of more than a few years of peace. He was surrounded by slaughter and carnage in fierce battles to the death. In his day, military commanders did not lead from the rear. Much of the time, Mormon was in the front lines, in deadly personal combat. That he even survived is amazing enough. That he survived to accomplish all he did is miraculous!

At age fifteen Mormon was called to serve his country as a leader of armies. He wrote, "And notwithstanding I being young, was large in stature; therefore the people of Nephi appointed me that I should be their leader, or the leader of their armies. Therefore it came to pass that in my sixteenth year I did go forth at the head of an army of the Nephites" (Mormon 2:1–2).

One might appropriately wonder what personal qualities would have been evident in a boy at age fifteen that would have led to his appointment so early as a military commander. He credits himself only with being of a sober mind and large in stature. But this was no ordinary boy. Several years earlier, the prophet Ammaron, keeper of the sacred records, had perceived that he was "a sober child, and . . . quick to observe" (Mormon 1:2). Ammaron had entrusted him with the secret of the hidden plates, which included a large volume of inscribed histories written over nine centuries, as well as the brass plates from

Jerusalem and certain sacred relics. He had been identified as the Lord's historian several years before he was old enough to command armies.

At age fifteen he had also been favored with a personal visitation from the Lord himself. He had a great work to do in this hostile world. We may safely assume that the Savior had known Mormon, as he had known the prophet Jeremiah, long before he was born on the earth. Assuredly, he was brought to the earth at this time for a purpose. To fulfill this purpose, he would be both a warrior and a prophet.

Fourteen centuries later, Mormon would play a central role in the life of another sober-minded boy—Joseph Smith—who also lived in a hostile world, and who saw the Savior and received a dramatic assignment during his fifteenth year.

For some reason, when Mormon was eleven years old, his father moved his family south to the land of Zarahemla. Soon thereafter, a major war broke out. Almost certainly, Mormon would have been drawn into the conflict and would have gained his first experience as a soldier at about age twelve. No doubt his service was outstanding. His physical strength, his courage, and his leadership abilities were such that before his sixteenth birthday, he was leading men into battle. Soon he was the commander of armies of thirty thousand soldiers and more.

Success did not come immediately. For the first three years of his military career he knew only defeat. His frightened armies retreated northward, taking refuge in the city of Angola, which they fortified as best they could, but they were driven out. Further defeats followed. Even a seasoned veteran might have been discouraged. But finally, with an army of forty-two thousand, he defeated an enemy army of similar size.

He became a brilliant military leader. Once, twenty years into his military career, he sadly noted, "Nevertheless the strength of the Lord was not with us; yea, we were left to ourselves, that the Spirit of the Lord did not abide in us; therefore we had become weak like unto our brethren" (Mormon 2:26). Yet with such an army, numbering only thirty thousand troops, he soundly defeated a Lamanite army of fifty thousand. This kind of success was repeated over and over as his armies dwindled and the end of their civilization drew near.

Mormon was called to lead a nation of renegades. It would have been more fitting for this noble soldier to have led a victorious army composed of men of valor and high purpose. Instead, he knew from the start he was engaged in a failing cause. He also knew why their cause would fail. His soldiers fought for unrighteous goals. They were confirmed in their wicked ways and would not repent. They wanted to be saved in their wickedness, not from it.

One of the constant vexations in his military life was the everlasting presence of the Gadianton robbers. He would often lament their destructive influence on his people. This band, with their secret oaths and covenants, grew steadily more powerful as the people of Nephi grew steadily more wicked. The wickedness of the Gadiantons and the Nephite people they influenced was inexcusable when they rebelled willfully and knowingly against the Lord. It is one thing to sin because of the weakness of our faith, but quite another when we know God but choose to follow Satan. "Now they did not sin ignorantly, for they knew the will of God concerning them, for it had been taught unto them; therefore they did willfully rebel against God" (3 Nephi 6:18).

Although Mormon was a military man, he was first and foremost a prophet. When he wrote of his life as a warrior, he spoke in the words of a prophet. He never stopped hoping that his people would return to the Lord and live for his blessings. He hoped their mourning and lamentation, when they were faced with destruction, would signal the softening of their hearts and their repentance. But it was not to be. He lamented:

> But behold this my joy was vain, for their sorrowing was not unto repentance, because of the goodness of God; but it was rather the sorrowing of the damned, because the Lord would not always suffer them to take happiness in sin.
>
> And they did not come unto Jesus with broken hearts and contrite spirits, but they did curse God, and wish to die. (Mormon 2:13–14)
>
> Behold, I had led them, notwithstanding their wickedness I had led them many times to battle, and had loved them, according to the love of God which was in me, with all my heart; and my soul had been poured out in prayer unto my God all the day long for them; nevertheless, it was without faith, because of the hardness of their hearts. (Mormon 3:12)

Some military commanders are in that profession because they enjoy the thrill of warfare; Mormon never did. He was a man of God.

He lamented the sorry fate of his people. He strove relentlessly to teach them lessons of peace. He mourned over the loss of his warriors. In the end, he died a lonely and brokenhearted leader, but he was never defeated as a man.

The noble qualities of this military man, which at first resulted in his being chosen to lead the Nephite armies, also gave him the power to save them repeatedly from the destruction they ultimately experienced. He was large and powerful physically. He was intellectually brilliant and dedicated completely to the cause of truth and right. He was motivated by the highest ideals of patriotism. His desire was to serve his people and save them from destruction, both physically and spiritually. He was a righteous man and was aided constantly by the power of the Holy Ghost.

A striking feature of his written record is the attention he gave to one heroic military figure of an earlier day. As Mormon abridged the voluminous records placed in his care, large periods of time often had to be covered in a few chapters or even a few verses. But one era was covered in impressive detail. This was the lengthy military campaign led by Captain Moroni several centuries before Mormon's time. For twenty chapters, he retold the story of this heroic Nephite leader.

This first Moroni was a man after Mormon's own heart. Here was a man who, like himself, had been called to command armies in his early youth, one who was expected to save his nation in great peril, one who was devoted to his religion, his country, his family. This Moroni rent his clothes and raised the title of liberty throughout the land, rallying his people in defense of "our God, our religion, and freedom, and our peace, our wives and our children" (Alma 46:12).

Both Mormon and the first Moroni lived and breathed military strategy, battle, victory, and defeat. Both were dedicated patriots. Love of country and fighting for freedom and family were part and parcel of their religion. Above all, they were men of integrity. Mormon's eloquent tribute to Moroni is a fitting definition of Mormon himself. He wrote:

> Moroni was a strong and a mighty man; he was a man of a perfect understanding; yea, a man that did not delight in bloodshed; a man whose soul did joy in the liberty and the freedom of his country, and his brethren from bondage and slavery;
> Yea, a man whose heart did swell with thanksgiving to his God,

for the many privileges and blessings which he bestowed upon his people; a man who did labor exceedingly for the welfare and safety of his people.

Yea, and he was a man who was firm in the faith of Christ, and he had sworn with an oath to defend his people, his rights, and his country, and his religion, even to the loss of his blood. . . .

Yea, verily, verily I say unto you, if all men had been, and were, and ever would be, like unto Moroni, behold, the very powers of hell would have been shaken forever; yea, the devil would never have power over the hearts of the children of men. (Alma 48:11–13, 17)

Mormon was also that kind of man. All of these things could be said of him as well. Mormon saw in Moroni a kindred spirit whom he could recommend as an example to follow. And when it came time to name his own son, he chose for him the name Moroni.

At one point, faithful Mormon gave up on his stubborn and unrepentant countrymen and for ten years refused to lead them. Because of their "wickedness and abomination" he "did utterly refuse from this time forth to be a commander and leader of this people" (Mormon 3:11). But, notwithstanding this decision, sometime at about age sixty-five, fifty years after his first call to military service, Mormon again went to battle: "But behold, I was without hope, for I knew the judgments of the Lord which should come upon them; for they repented not of their iniquities, but did struggle for their lives without calling upon that Being who had created them" (Mormon 5:2).

Mormon wrote to his son, Moroni, and described in agonizing terms the scene of horror that he saw.

O the depravity of my people! They are without order and without mercy. Behold, I am but a man, and I have but the strength of a man, and I cannot any longer enforce my commands.

And they have become strong in their perversion; and they are alike brutal, sparing none, neither old nor young; and they delight in everything save that which is good; and the suffering of our women and our children upon all the face of this land doth exceed everything; yea, tongue cannot tell, neither can it be written. (Moroni 9:18–19)

The situation seemed desperate and hopeless, the evil of his enemies overwhelming.

The Lamanites have many prisoners, which they took from the tower of Sherrizah; and there were men, women, and children.

And the husbands and fathers of those women and children they have slain; and they feed the women upon the flesh of their husbands, and the children upon the flesh of their fathers; and no water, save a little, do they give unto them.

And notwithstanding this great abomination of the Lamanites, it doth not exceed that of our people in Moriantum. For behold, many of the daughters of the Lamanites have they taken prisoners; and after depriving them of that which was most dear and precious above all things, which is chastity and virtue—

And after they had done this thing, they did murder them in a most cruel manner, torturing their bodies even unto death; and after they have done this, they devour their flesh like unto wild beasts, because of the hardness of their hearts; and they do it for a token of bravery. (Moroni 9:7–10)

With diminished hope but undiminished loyalty, Mormon continued to lead his warriors—sometimes to victory, more often to retreat from the onrushing hordes of Lamanites. He mourned as both the Lamanites and Nephites descended into hopeless savagery and brutality, and he wrote his history as a testament to the fate of all who forsake righteousness.

It is impossible for the tongue to describe, or for man to write a perfect description of the horrible scene of the blood and carnage which was among the people, both of the Nephites and of the Lamanites; and every heart was hardened, so that they delighted in the shedding of blood continually.

And there never had been so great wickedness among all the children of Lehi, nor even among all the house of Israel, according to the words of the Lord, as was among this people. (Mormon 4:11–12)

Finally, the dreadful day arrived when the overwhelming legions of Lamanites could be held back no longer. The valiant but old and weakened Mormon fought with his waning strength at the head of his army, as ten thousand after ten thousand fell to their deaths around him on the plains of Cumorah.

It was an aged and wounded warrior who wrote in the seventy-fifth year of his life that he had personally led his men and wielded his sword in the final battle and had survived with a group of only twenty-four, including his son, Moroni. It was a venerable military commander, weighed down nearly unto death with sorrow for his people, who one last time had taken his people into battle. They had been "led in the front by [him]" (Mormon 6:11). For one final time, he had served these people who wanted only to be saved in their wickedness.

After this final battle, Mormon recorded the sad statistics and described the awful scene. In this last struggle, he had lost 23 commanders, each with their 10,000 men. Approximately 230,000 men perished in this final, cataclismic day, which marked the end of the once-proud Nephite nation. Mormon himself had been badly wounded, was thought to be dead, and had been passed over by the savage hordes as they completed their slaughter.

Weary beyond description with the weight of this and a hundred other battles, and sick from the scene of desolation all around him, he recorded his poignant lamentation:

> My soul was rent with anguish, because of the slain of my people, and I cried: O ye fair ones, how could ye have departed from the ways of the Lord! O ye fair ones, how could ye have rejected that Jesus, who stood with open arms to receive you! Behold, if ye had not done this, ye would not have fallen. But behold, ye are fallen, and I mourn your loss. O ye fair sons and daughters, ye fathers and mothers, ye husbands and wives, ye fair ones, how is it that ye could have fallen! But behold, ye are gone, and my sorrows cannot bring your return. . . .
>
> O that ye had repented before this great destruction had come upon you. But behold, ye are gone, and the Father, yea, the Eternal Father of heaven, knoweth your state; and he doeth with you according to his justice and mercy. (Mormon 6:16–20, 22)

Mormon was seventy-four years old at the last battle, in AD 385, having been born in AD 311 (see Mormon 1:6). In AD 401, Moroni announced the death of his father, which may have occurred only recently (see Mormon 8:3, 6). He may, therefore, have lived to be eighty-nine or ninety—an amazing age, considering the time in which he lived and the dangerous life he led. He did not die of an illness, or of old age, but was killed in battle by prowling Lamanites.

Mormon had prayed that his son would live faithfully to see the final end of his people and to make a record of it. Moroni was true to his father's trust.

*chapter three*

# THE HISTORIAN

While serving as a soldier, Mormon searched and studied the record of his people and wrote a classic abridgement of their one-thousand-year history.

Why did Mormon write? He certainly had enough to do otherwise! As the Lord's prophet, he had been commanded to write. Yet he lived in an environment that was anything but congenial to the kind of research and study required to produce a master literary work. To say he was distracted would be a major understatement. How could he write at all? How could he find the opportunity to concentrate and ponder upon his writing? How could he successfully abridge a mountain of cumbersome records when he and his armies were being constantly chased, harassed, and slaughtered?

How could Mormon so gracefully synthesize the complex story of several cultures into a cohesive record? More remarkable still, how could he, with great accuracy and consistency, distill from this voluminous record "the fulness of the everlasting Gospel" (JS—History 1:34)? This was his main task.

The gospel of Jesus Christ is not a simple theology. Yet, in Mormon's writing of it, he left nothing undone and still retained the essential simplicity of its doctrine, with all of its beauty and refinement and tenderness. The result of his effort was a single, near-perfect work, written so successfully that it would stand the scrutiny of the harshest critics for generations and emerge unscathed. Think about it! It is truly a marvelous work and a wonder.

Mormon introduced himself and described the central focus of his mission in these words:

> And behold, I am called Mormon, being called after the land of Mormon, the land in which Alma did establish the church among the people, yea, the first church which was established among them after their transgression.
>
> Behold, I am a disciple of Jesus Christ, the Son of God. I have been called of him to declare his word among his people, that they might have everlasting life. . . .
>
> Therefore I do make my record from the accounts which have been given by those who were before me, until the commencement of my day;
>
> And then I do make a record of the things which I have seen with mine own eyes. (3 Nephi 5:12–13, 16–17)

In about the year AD 321, when Mormon was a child of ten, Ammaron, the current keeper of the Nephite history, sought him out and gave him responsibility for his huge collection of records (see Mormon 1:2–4). These covered both the secular and the religious history of the Nephite nation for hundreds of years. It included Laban's brass plates, containing the family history and much of the Old Testament. It also included the record of the Jaredite people since their departure from the Tower of Babel. We must remember that these were not contained on lightweight computer discs, but on heavy metal plates. Ammoron had hidden these records away in a cave for their protection from the raging anarchy. In this cave they would be secure until Mormon was older. But it was indeed unusual for a ten-year-old boy to be asked to assume this kind of responsibility.

How did Mormon, the sober young boy and later the mighty warrior, become Mormon the great historian? There is no specific account of Mormon's receiving a call from the Lord. But his work must have originated with such a call; Mormon makes this very clear. He was a man with a mission. He was driven to accomplish this mission under the harshest circumstances and by the urgency of knowing that the civilization collapsing around him would soon be destroyed. Without his work, the priceless record of their history would have been lost.

Some might characterize Mormon primarily as a historian. This is not accurate. But he was, indeed, a great historian. He was an outstanding keeper of history, having possession of an archive of one thousand years of sacred and secular records. He was a most unusual writer of history, having selected and abridged the portions of these extensive records that seemed most pertinent to his purpose. Finally, he was an astute interpreter of history. He was not only a most perceptive student and scholar but, above all else, a prophet of God. Mormon not only interpreted the significance of those thousand years of history, but he did so with a grand purpose, under the direct command of the Lord. So, amid the terrible distractions of a prolonged war, this commander of the armies kept his focus clearly upon his greater mission.

There are implicit difficulties in accurately writing or abridging history. Along with the usual difficulties, Mormon had a few additional problems. Besides the distractions of his military life, which caused all kinds of interruptions, he was working with a difficult medium: a stylus and golden plates. Golden plates did not come with a delete button to facilitate editing and correcting. What was written had to be right the first time. No rewrites, no corrections, no second thoughts. This may account for the awkward phrasing in some of his paragraphs.

Mormon's interpretation of what happened and where and why would be critically examined by antagonistic scholars in ages to come and must pass the test. But it would not be possible to reconsider or amend what had been said. Under the circumstances he faced, most authors would be pressed to describe accurately and succinctly the events of the previous one hundred years. Mormon wrote accurately and succinctly about the previous one thousand years!

Those years covered a lot of time and territory. There were three or four distinct cultures. There were changes in governments and styles of governing within and between the cultures. There was evolution in patterns of living and of speech.

But the greater purpose of his writing added another dimension of difficulty. He was commanded to write the complete gospel of Jesus Christ. In his historical narrative he discussed not just a few interesting aspects of the doctrine of Christ but virtually all of it. In doing so, he synthesized the teachings and preachings of many earlier prophets, each of whom taught in their own style and with a variety of objectives. He was faithful to what they said and to what they meant. And he did it all without the luxury of any excuse for misinterpretation, exaggeration, omission, or confusion. Mormon's book had to contain the pure doctrine of Christ, presented without error. And it does! The pure, constant, simple truths of the Savior's teachings came through without adulteration.

This book has been described by Joseph Smith as the most correct book on earth. No one has proven otherwise.

Offsetting his great disadvantages in writing, Mormon had some notable advantages. Unlike many writers of ancient history, he spoke the language of the people he wrote about. He understood the origins of his people and their history. He had the unusual benefit of holding in his hands the entire written record of the people of whom he wrote—of being able to read and reread, ponder and pray about its significance and then to edit and summarize it into one comprehensive volume.

There were other advantages of Mormon's calling as a prophet. He knew the causes of the problems described in the record and he even knew of the cultures' futures. As had Moses of old, he had seen in vision the past of which he wrote. Furthermore, as he wrote to us and for our day, we can be sure that he, as did his son, Moroni, saw us and our day in vision (see Mormon 8:35).

Since Mormon saw our day, he knew our dangers, and he wrote to save us from the disaster he witnessed among his own people. He identified the root causes of the downfall of his people and warned against them. In this aspect, Mormon's history is a prophetic history. He was called of God to write it, to point out its pitfalls. He was inspired of the Holy Spirit. Thus, his writing is scripture—the word of God.

Because of his prophetic insights, it was possible for him to describe not only what the ancient Nephites did but also what they thought and felt. He wrote as though he were a first-person witness to this history, from beginning to end. To aid him in his task, Mormon had the direct inspiration of the Lord and the assistance of angels. Mormon was not a scholar. He was a prophet. Even if Mormon were not accepted as a prophet, his work would still be a monumental one. But he was a prophet, and his work is a masterpiece.

Mormon took great pains to state exactly what the Lord intended to accomplish through him. We have, in these unusual explanations, a revelation of how an inspired man receives his "marching orders" from the Lord. As he left off abridging the record and came to the account of his own life and work, Mormon made the following comprehensive statement of three purposes for which he wrote:

Therefore I write unto you, Gentiles, and also unto you, house of Israel. . . .

Yea, behold, I write unto all the ends of the earth; yea, unto you, twelve tribes of Israel. . . .

And I write also unto the remnant of this people. . . .

And for this cause I write unto you, that ye may know that ye must all stand before the judgment-seat of Christ, yea, every soul who belongs to the whole human family of Adam; and ye must stand to be judged of your works, whether they be good or evil;

And also that ye may believe the gospel of Jesus Christ, which ye shall have among you; and also that the Jews, the covenant people of the Lord, shall have other witness besides him whom they saw and heard, that Jesus, whom they slew, was the very Christ and the very God. (Mormon 3:17–21)

In summary, Mormon's three main purposes in writing were (1) that we may know that every one of us must be judged of Christ, (2) that we may learn to believe in the gospel of Christ, and (3) that the Jews might have a second witness of Christ.

As he drew near to the close of his work, Mormon paused repeatedly to emphasize his mission. He was saying, "Listen to me. This is important. I'm not trying to entertain you. Satan is cunning and cruel and he is after you. He will try to destroy you, as he did my people. In order to avoid their fate, you must hearken unto our God. You must keep his commandments. You must avoid the big mistakes that others have made. Listen to me. Repent." He wrote:

O ye Gentiles, how can ye stand before the power of God, except ye shall repent and turn from your evil ways?

Know ye not that ye are in the hands of God? Know ye not that he hath all power, and at his great command the earth shall be rolled together as a scroll?

Therefore, repent ye, and humble yourselves before him, lest he shall come out in justice against you—lest a remnant of the seed of Jacob shall go forth among you as a lion, and tear you in pieces, and there is none to deliver. (Mormon 5:22–24)

Mormon gave us a brief account of the ministry of the Savior on the American continent. He would have liked to give us more, and would have, were it not that he was forbidden by the Lord. The Lord's reasons for limiting the account of the ministry of the Savior presents readers of the Book of Mormon with a challenge:

> And when [this people] shall have received this, which is expedient that they should have first, to try their faith, and if it shall so be that they shall believe these things then shall the greater things be made manifest unto them.
>
> And if it so be that they will not believe these things, then shall the greater things be withheld from them, unto their condemnation.
>
> Behold, I was about to write them, all which were engraven upon the plates of Nephi, but the Lord forbade it, saying: I will try the faith of my people.
>
> Therefore I, Mormon, do write the things which have been commanded me of the Lord. (3 Nephi 26:9–12)

A final explanation about the purpose of Mormon's record is found in the Words of Mormon. This brief chapter is found early in the Book of Mormon but was inserted as he was concluding his work, when he was pressed by the Spirit to add it. It seems to have been written almost as an afterthought. But the writings in 1 Nephi, which were then included, turned out to be a most wonderful addition to our present Book of Mormon. Always obedient to the Lord, Mormon explains:

> Wherefore, I chose these things [the writings of Nephi and Jacob], to finish my record upon them, which remainder of my record I shall take from the plates of Nephi; and I cannot write the hundredth part of the things of my people.
>
> But behold, I shall take these plates, which contain these prophesyings and revelations, and put them with the remainder of my record, for they are choice unto me; and I know they will be choice unto my brethren.
>
> And I do this for a wise purpose; for thus it whispereth me, according to the workings of the Spirit of the Lord which is in me. And now, I do not know all things; but the Lord knoweth all things which are to come; wherefore, he worketh in me to do according to his will. (Words of Mormon 1:5–7)

Members of the Church are aware of the meaning of the phrase "for a wise purpose" as Mormon used it here. The Lord anticipated, many hundreds of years in advance, the need for a backup record to replace the early pages of the manuscript that were translated by Joseph Smith and subsequently lost by Martin Harris. How grateful we are for the rich treasures contained in 1 and 2 Nephi and Jacob.

Mormon freely interpreted what he saw and wrote. Sometimes he drew conclusions or object lessons by using the phrase "And thus we see . . ." Other times he simply affirmed what seemed obvious from the story, expressing approval or disapproval. He often paused in his narrative to insert an editorial comment or brief dissertation so that readers would not miss the point. Sometimes he inserted a prophet's whole sermon or a letter to his son, which made a point of doctrine or truth. Fortunately, Mormon's son, Moroni, later included some of his father's finest writings about good and evil, faith, hope, charity, and the baptism of infants. The wonder of it is that these prophetic writings were made from the unlikely perspective of a commander of armies engaged in a ferocious, wicked, bloody war of extermination.

Mighty Mormon was as great in his writing of history as he was in commanding armies. No, he was greater. Because, as great as he was in warfare, warfare could never save his people. His writings have saved many—and will yet save many more who will hearken unto the call of the Savior to come unto him!

*chapter four*
# THE PROPHET

Mormon is such a diverse personality and his life's work so vast, it is likely that faithful readers of the Book of Mormon have differing perceptions of who and what he really was. We have considered his unique roles as a soldier and as a historian. Notwithstanding his great work in these areas, it is clear that Mormon's chief mission in his life was first, last, and always as a prophet of the Lord Jesus Christ.

Mormon's two other careers, soldier and historian, were always in context with this third and most important calling in life. All that he did as a soldier and all that he wrote as a historian was under the mantle and in the words of a prophet.

The Lord's prophets have always had as their chief commission to testify of the divine mission of the Savior Jesus Christ. They are his representatives on this earth. The Book of Mormon, for which Mormon was largely responsible, is a testament of Jesus Christ. With the panorama of history related in the book and all the lessons of life taught in its pages, the central figure is still the Savior Jesus Christ. It is a book about him, about his gospel, his teachings, his people, and his plan. The book is written by his chosen prophet for his own purposes:

> Hearken, O ye Gentiles, and hear the words of Jesus Christ, the Son of the living God, which he hath commanded me that I should speak concerning you, for, behold he commandeth me that I should write, saying:
>
> Turn, all ye Gentiles, from your wicked ways; and repent of your evil doings, of your lyings and deceivings, and of your whoredoms,

and of your secret abominations, and your idolatries, and of your murders, and your priestcrafts, and your envyings, and your strifes, and
from all your wickedness and abominations, and come unto me, and
be baptized in my name, that ye may receive a remission of your sins,
and be filled with the Holy Ghost, that ye may be numbered with my
people who are of the house of Israel. (3 Nephi 30:1–2)

Even faithful readers of the Book of Mormon might be surprised
to discover just how many references there are to Christ in this book.
In some missions of the Church, the elders and sisters have been chal-
lenged to read straight through the book and to mark in red each refer-
ence they find about the Savior. Surprisingly, this exercise has resulted
in the discovery of over five thousand separate instances in which the
Savior is mentioned or quoted! Scarcely a chapter exists that does not
refer significantly to him. Readers might benefit from this exercise in
their own families.

Mormon selected, compiled, and abridged most of the book that
bears his name. What was his main concern as he prepared this volume
to be read by future generations?

His theme, his purpose, and his hope was that we, his latter-day
brothers and sisters, would accept the gospel of Jesus Christ and live by
his teachings. He thought of us as his own people, he worried about
our well-being, and he taught the principles that would save us from
sorrow and destruction. Mormon's life was lived with us in mind. He
wrote as though he were speaking to us. In all this, he was the classic
prophet of God. We honor him in that role!

How and when he was called to be the Lord's prophet, we do not
know; he did not say. But he clearly and repeatedly announced that he
had been called: "Behold, I am a disciple of Jesus Christ, the Son of God.
I have been called of him to declare his word among his people, that
they might have everlasting life" (3 Nephi 5:13). His mission from the
very beginning extended far beyond his own people. He was to write of
Christ to the remnant of the Nephites and Lamanites, to the Jews, and to
all the house of Israel and to the Gentiles—in fact, to the whole world.

Therefore I write unto you, Gentiles, and also unto you, house of
Israel, when the work shall commence, that ye shall be about to prepare to return to the land of your inheritance;

Yea, behold, I write unto all the ends of the earth; yea, unto you,
twelve tribes of Israel, who shall be judged according to your works

by the twelve whom Jesus chose to be his disciples in the land of Jerusalem.

And I write also unto the remnant of this people, who shall also be judged by the twelve whom Jesus chose in this land. (Mormon 3:17–19)

Mormon and the first latter-day prophet, Joseph Smith, both had the remarkable privilege of seeing the Savior when each was only fifteen. Mormon wrote, "And I, being fifteen years of age and being somewhat of a sober mind, therefore I was visited of the Lord, and tasted and knew of the goodness of Jesus" (Mormon 1:15). One can imagine that the Lord's message to Mormon at that time was similar to the one given by Moroni to Joseph Smith: "God has a work for you to do" (JS—History 1:33). But, as with young Joseph, Mormon first had to prepare. Mormon's first instinct after being visited by the Savior was to preach to the people. But it wasn't yet time for that. He wrote, "And I did endeavor to preach unto this people, but my mouth was shut, and I was forbidden that I should preach unto them; for behold they had wilfully rebelled against their God; and the beloved disciples were taken away out of the land, because of their iniquity. But I did remain among them, but I was forbidden to preach unto them, because of the hardness of their hearts; and because of the hardness of their hearts the land was cursed for their sake" (Mormon 1:16–17).

Within a few months of his vision of the Savior, Mormon was called to the service of his country, to become a leader of its armies. Soon thereafter, he took possession of the sacred records. Finally, he was given the full authority of the Lord's prophet.

In about AD 360 there was a period of ten years free of major battles (Mormon 3:1). Mormon turned his attention to preparations for more war. But it was also a time when he could devote himself to a major effort to bring his people to repentance so that further war might be avoided. The result of his efforts, as it was so often, was a great disappointment.

And it came to pass that the Lamanites did not come to battle again until ten years more had passed away. And behold, I had employed my people, the Nephites, in preparing their lands and their arms against the time of battle.

And it came to pass that the Lord did say unto me: Cry unto this people—Repent ye, and come unto me, and be ye baptized, and build up again my church, and ye shall be spared.

> And I did cry unto this people, but it was in vain; and they did not
> realize that it was the Lord that had spared them, and granted unto
> them a chance for repentance. And behold they did harden their hearts
> against the Lord their God. (Mormon 3:1–3)

He was constantly faced with this problem so typical in the experience of other prophets—this hardness of the hearts of the people. The
Nephites seemed more rebellious than anyone. He did everything for
them that an inspired leader could, but they would not listen. When
they were victorious in battle, they gave themselves the credit. When
they were defeated, they sought only revenge. They seemed incor-
rigible. After many years, they had become so stubborn, willful, and
wicked that their leader grew entirely discouraged with trying to save
them. But he never stopped loving them.

A characteristic of true prophets of God is that they never give up.
Think of the Old Testament prophets who sealed their testimonies
with their blood. Think of the apostles of Christ, who did the same.
Think of Abinadi and Alma and Moroni and of the Prophet Joseph
Smith, whose lives were never free of sorrow and disappointment,
but who carried on to the very end of their lives. Mormon was no
different.

After those ten years of peace, they went again to war to defend
against invading Lamanites. Under Mormon's leadership, they were
victorious. "They began to boast in their own strength, and began
to swear before the heavens that they would avenge themselves of the
blood of their brethren who had been slain by their enemies. And they
did swear by the heavens, and also by the throne of God, that they
would go up to battle against their enemies, and would cut them off
from the face of the land" (Mormon 3:9–10).

As he saw the events of those times unfolding, it was all according
to the formula he had been taught: Righteousness brings blessings;
unrighteousness brings trouble. If only he could change their destiny
by getting the people to repent! But he could not. They would not
repent. So he watched the horrible drama unfold and stood in another
role of prophets, as a living witness, and recorded the unfolding trag-
edy for the benefit of future generations.

> And I did stand as an idle witness to manifest unto the world
> the things which I saw and heard, according to the manifestations

of the Spirit had which testified of things to come. . . .

And these things doth the Spirit manifest unto me; therefore I write unto you all. (Mormon 3:16, 20)

[My people] were once a delightsome people, and they had Christ for their shepherd; yea, they were led even by God the Father.

But now, behold, they are led about by Satan, even as chaff is driven before the wind, or as a vessel is tossed about upon the waves, without sail or anchor, or without anything wherewith to steer her; and even as she is, so are they. (Mormon 5:17–18)

And now, behold, I would speak somewhat unto the remnant of this people who are spared, if it so be that God may give unto them my words, that they may know of the things of their fathers; yea, I speak unto you, ye remnant of the house of Israel; and these are the words which I speak:

Know ye that ye are of the house of Israel.

Know ye that ye must come unto repentance, or ye cannot be saved.

Know ye that ye must lay down your weapons of war, and delight no more in the shedding of blood, and take them not again, save it be that God shall command you.

Know ye that ye must come to the knowledge of your fathers, and repent of all your sins and iniquities, and believe in Jesus Christ, that he is the Son of God. . . .

Therefore repent, and be baptized in the name of Jesus, and lay hold upon the gospel of Christ, which shall be set before you, not only in this record but also in the record which shall come unto the Gentiles from the Jews, which record shall come from the Gentiles unto you.

For behold, this is written for the intent that ye may believe that; and if ye believe that ye will believe this also; and if ye believe this ye will know concerning your fathers, and also the marvelous works which were wrought by the power of God among them.

And ye will also know that ye are a remnant of the seed of Jacob; therefore ye are numbered among the people of the first covenant; and if it so be that ye believe in Christ, and are baptized, first with water, then with fire and with the Holy Ghost, following the example of our Savior, according to that which he hath commanded us, it shall be well with you in the day of judgment. Amen. (Mormon 7:1–5, 8–10)

We do not know how long Mormon lived after the great, final battle of Cumorah. He was badly wounded but recovered and wrote of the pathetic end of decades of war. His words are poignant. Readers can imagine the deep feelings of this prophet's broken heart as he lay wounded, lonesome, sick, and weary unto death, and lamented over the unimaginable loss of a whole civilization: "My soul was rent with anguish, because of the slain of my people, and I cried: . . . O ye fair ones, how could ye have rejected that Jesus, who stood with open arms to receive you! . . . But behold, ye are fallen, and I mourn your loss. . . . O ye fair sons and daughters . . . fathers . . . mothers . . . ye fair ones, how is it that ye could have fallen! . . . But behold, ye are gone, and my sorrows cannot bring your return" (Mormon 6:16–20).

*chapter five*

# THE FATHER

In earlier chapters, emphasis was given to mighty Mormon as a warrior, as a historian, and as a prophet. Under the stressful and distracting circumstances of his life, it would not be surprising if he had been unable to give much attention to family matters. Indeed, his writings include little mention of his family except for one son, Moroni. Most likely his own family suffered the fate of so many other Nephites and was lost in the cataclysmic warfare.

Moroni outlived all the rest of the family and naturally had a close relationship with his father. Mormon's attention to his son reveals a true father in the best sense. His relationship with Moroni tells us something about both men and is worthy of special mention here.

The careers of some busy men become so all-consuming that their roles as fathers suffer. Mormon's concurrent involvement in three major careers could easily have had such a result, but it did not. Instead, his deep love for his son, his solicitous concern for his welfare, his fatherly counsel, and his careful instruction stand out in the pages he wrote as worthy examples for all his readers. In the concluding pages of the Book of Mormon we read of a man whose son was always on his mind and in his prayers.

It was mentioned in an earlier chapter that Mormon chose a special name for his son—a choice apparently inspired by a great and much-admired military hero—Captain Moroni, familiar to us for his title of liberty (Alma 46:12–13, 18–20). Mormon's lavish tribute to Captain Moroni attests to his nobility and tells us of the hopes Mormon had for the son to whom he gave that name (Alma 48:11–18). Mormon's son lived up to his name. In the account of the final calamity at Cumorah, he is listed with his father as one of the commanders of ten thousand soldiers (Mormon 6:11–12).

Fifteen years after that final battle, as Moroni resumed his own writings, his words contained a subtle tribute to the mutual respect that had existed between father and son: "I have but few things to write, which things I have been commanded by my father. . . . Behold, my father was also killed by [Lamanites], and I even remain alone to write the sad tale of the destruction of my people. But behold, they are gone, and I fulfill the commandment of my father. And whether they will slay me, I know not" (Mormon 8:1, 3, 6). Moroni's regard for his father is further attested to in his stirring testimony in chapters 8 and 9 of Mormon. Here he demonstrates the character of a son who was not only a great teacher in his own right but true to his father's teachings.

Soon after Moroni's call to the ministry, Mormon had written him a letter, which Moroni saved and included with his own plates. Notice the tender words of a concerned father, upset about false doctrine creeping into the Church:

> My beloved son, Moroni, I rejoice exceedingly that your Lord Jesus Christ hath been mindful of you, and hath called you to his ministry, and to his holy work.
>
> I am mindful of you always in my prayers, continually praying unto God the Father in the name of his Holy Child, Jesus, that he, through his infinite goodness and grace, will keep you through the endurance of faith on his name to the end.
>
> And now, my son, I speak unto you concerning that which grieveth me exceedingly; for it grieveth me that there should disputations rise among you.
>
> For, if I have learned the truth, there have been disputations among you concerning the baptism of your little children.
>
> And now, my son, I desire that ye should labor diligently, that this gross error should be removed from among you. (Moroni 8:2–6)

Then follows a tender closing: "Farewell, my son, until I shall write unto you, or shall meet you again. Amen" (Moroni 8:30).

Several other poignant passages are found in a second letter, written much later but likewise preserved by Moroni. Here Mormon is grieving over the stubborn wickedness of his people but concludes with a wonderful admonition to his son, which all could take to heart:

> My beloved son, I write to you again that ye may know that I am yet alive; but I write somewhat of that which is grievous.
>
> For behold, I have had a sore battle with the Lamanites, in which we did not conquer; and Archeantus has fallen by the sword, and also Luram and Emron; yea, and we have lost a great number of our choice men.
>
> And now behold, my son, I fear lest the Lamanites shall destroy this people; for they do not repent, and Satan stirreth them up continually to anger one with another.
>
> Behold, I am laboring with them continually; and when I speak the word of God with sharpness they tremble and anger against me; and when I use no sharpness they harden their hearts against it; wherefore, I fear lest the Spirit of the Lord hath ceased striving with them.
>
> For so exceedingly do they anger that it seemeth me that they have no fear of death; and they have lost their love, one towards another; and they thirst after blood and revenge continually.
>
> And now, my beloved son, notwithstanding their hardness, let us labor diligently; for if we should cease to labor, we should be brought under condemnation; for we have a labor to perform whilst in this tabernacle of clay, that we may conquer the enemy of all righteousness, and rest our souls in the kingdom of God. (Moroni 9:1–6)

Further in this final letter we see a sorrowing prophet taking his trusted son into his confidence, to share in some measure the burden of his heart. He describes the dreadful cruelty of both the Nephite and Lamanite armies. Then he confides to his son his agony in their inhumanity: "O my beloved son, how can a people like this, that are without civilization—(And only a few years have passed away, and they were a civil and delightsome people) But O my son, how can a people like this, whose delight is in so much abomination—How can we expect that God will stay his hand in judgement against us? Behold, my heart cries: Wo unto this people. Come out in judgement, O God, and hide their sins, and wickedness, and abominations from before thy face!" (Moroni 9:11–15).

Finally, after giving an account of the deplorable state of his decadent people, Mormon confesses that he can no longer recommend them to God. Notice in the following passages the tender love of a wonderful, noble father for his son:

> And now, my son, I dwell no longer upon this horrible scene. Behold, thou knowest the wickedness of this people; thou knowest that they are without principle, and past feeling; and their wickedness doth exceed that of the Lamanites.
>
> Behold, my son, I cannot recommend them unto God lest he should smite me.
>
> But, behold my son, I recommend thee unto God, and I trust in Christ that thou wilt be saved; and I pray unto God that he will spare thy life, to witness the return of his people unto him, or their utter destruction; for I know that they must perish except they repent and return unto him. . . .
>
> My son, be faithful in Christ; and may not the things which I have written grieve thee, to weigh thee down unto death; but may Christ lift thee up, and may his sufferings and death, and the showing his body unto our fathers, and his mercy and long-suffering, and the hope of his glory and of eternal life, rest in your mind forever.
>
> And may the grace of God the Father, whose throne is high in the heavens, and our Lord Jesus Christ, who sitteth on the right hand of his power, until all things shall become subject unto him, be, and abide with you forever. Amen. (Moroni 9:20–22, 25–26)

Again, behold the man!

PART TWO

# Mormon's
## TEACHINGS

*chapter six*

# THE TEACHER

The entire Book of Mormon represents the teachings of Mormon. It was Mormon who, under inspiration from heaven, selected the vital teachings he knew we needed from the sacred records he had available. The book is written mostly in his own words.

In presenting some of Mormon's significant teachings, I have left the words of the prophets other than Mormon to speak for themselves. The quotations chosen include only those from Mormon's own personal teachings and his own editorial comments. I have commented about some of the doctrines he taught, but I mostly have chosen to quote liberally from his own words. Mormon's powerful words reveal clearly the things that were especially dear to his heart. The reader is invited to savor these scriptural quotations, to read them carefully and ponder and appreciate them. They come from the heart of a great Christian man, and they carry important messages for our own time.

Being a commander of armies was undoubtedly the least fulfilling of Mormon's three careers. His whole purpose as a soldier, everything he did as a military man, was focused not only on defeating the enemy and saving his own people from death but on giving them a chance to repent and gain everlasting life. Unfortunately, in this he did not succeed.

Nor was he content simply to act as a historian, compiling history written by others. His objective in compiling the Book of Mormon was to teach the lessons of history and to encourage his readers to repent and come unto Christ.

Mormon was a prophet of the Lord. As a prophet, he preached repentance and taught righteousness. His major themes were these:

- *Freedom and equality.* Coming from a veteran soldier who served his country for so many years, it is not surprising to hear him speak much of these virtues and of duty to God and country.
- *The fountains and fruits of righteousness.* These are prosperity and happiness.
- *Pride and apostasy.* Ironically, these almost always followed periods of righteousness.
- *Conflict between good and evil.* There is a relentless war between the Savior and Lucifer.
- *Secret combinations.* Mormon clearly identified and warned against this satanic threat, which destroyed the Nephites and threatens even our own generation.
- *The great virtues.* These, among others, are humility, personal integrity, and morality.
- *Faith, hope, and charity.* At the end of his long life of warfare, Mormon's heart was still full of the pure love of Christ.
- *Repentance and coming unto Christ.* What could be more central to our existence here on earth?

As he wrote, Mormon used five methods to emphasize the things he felt were most important: (1) highlighting the teachings of others, (2) drawing lessons from the words of others, (3) inserting commentary, (4) including complete texts from others, and (5) adding his own discourses.

### Highlighting the teachings of others

One means of emphasis Mormon used was to feature events or teachings of others that demonstrate what brings people either to God or to destruction. For example, he referred extensively to the profound change of heart that occurred in the Lamanites who were converted by the sons of Mosiah (see Alma 19:33; 24:6–19).

### Drawing lessons from the words of others

Lest the reader miss an important point, after giving an account of some event, Mormon often used such phrases as "And thus we see . . ." or "Thus we can plainly discern . . ." followed by his timely advice. For example, "And thus we see that the Spirit of the Lord began to withdraw from the Nephites, because of the wickedness and the hardness of their hearts" (Helaman 6:35).

### Inserting commentary

Mormon often inserted into his narrative his own editorial emphasis. For example, he emphasized repeatedly that authority is required for one to minister for God.

> Now it came to pass after Abinadi had spoken these words that the people of king Noah durst not lay their hands on him, for the Spirit of the Lord was upon him; and his face shone with exceeding luster, even as Moses' did while in the mount of Sinai, while speaking with the Lord.
>
> And he spake with power and authority from God. (Mosiah 13:5–6)

> And it came to pass that Alma, having authority from God, ordained priests; . . . having been commanded of God. (Mosiah 18:18, 29)

> And it came to pass that king Limhi and many of his people were desirous to be baptized; but there was none in the land that had authority from God. And Ammon declined doing this thing, considering himself an unworthy servant. (Mosiah 21:33)

> None received authority to preach or to teach except it were by him from God. Therefore he consecrated all their priests and all their teachers; and none were consecrated except they were just men. (Mosiah 23:17)

### Including complete texts from others

Sometimes Mormon wanted us to hear the whole message of another prophet in the prophet's own words. Thus, he used quotations from others where he deemed these to be particularly useful or profound. The discourses of Alma and Amulek in the book of Alma are examples. The words of Alma to his sons (see Alma 36–42), Helaman's letter to Captain Moroni describing the miraculous fighting of the two thousand stripling warriors (see Alma 56), the correspondence between Captain Moroni and Pahoran (see Alma 60–61), King Benjamin's matchless address (see Mosiah 2–4), and Abinadi's fearless discourse (see Mosiah 12–16)—all of these contain sermons Mormon wanted us to read.

### Adding his own discourses

Fortunately, in a few instances, there are first-person sermons or writings from Mormon on favorite topics. For example, in chapter 28 of 3 Nephi, Mormon inserted twenty-six choice verses describing the unprecedented ministry of the Three Nephites and the reasons the work of these disciples was so important.

As Mormon gave his account of the apocalyptic destruction that followed the crucifixion of the Savior and wrote of Christ's ministry among the Nephites, he testified of the verity of all he had written. Mormon concluded with his account of Christ's Nephite ministry and his own ringing call to repentance. His testimony is emphatic, credible, and inspirational. In this we see the spiritual power of this man of God:

> And now, whoso readeth, let him understand; he that hath the scriptures, let him search them, and see and behold if all these deaths and destructions by fire, and by smoke, and by tempests, and by whirlwinds, and by the opening of the earth to receive them, and all these things are not unto the fulfilling of the prophecies of many of the holy prophets. . . .
>
> I will show unto you that the people of Nephi who were spared, and also those who had been called Lamanites, who had been spared, did have great favors shown unto them, and great blessings poured out upon their heads, insomuch that soon after the ascension of Christ into heaven he did truly manifest himself unto them—
>
> Showing his body unto them, and ministering unto them; and an account of his ministry shall be given hereafter. (3 Nephi 10:14, 18–19)

> Wo unto him that spurneth at the doings of the Lord; yea, wo unto him that shall deny the Christ and his works!
>
> Yea, wo unto him that shall deny the revelations of the Lord, and that shall say the Lord no longer worketh by revelation, or by prophecy, or by gifts, or by tongues, or by healings, or by the power of the Holy Ghost!
>
> Yea, and wo unto him that shall say at that day, to get gain, that there can be no miracle wrought by Jesus Christ; for he that doeth this shall become like unto the son of perdition, for whom there was no mercy, according to the word of Christ!
>
> Yea, and ye need not any longer hiss, nor spurn, nor make game of the Jews, nor any of the remnant of the house of Israel; for behold, the Lord remembereth his covenant unto them, and he will do unto them according to that which he hath sworn.
>
> Therefore ye need not suppose that ye can turn the right hand of the Lord unto the left, that he may not execute judgment unto

the fulfilling of the covenant which he hath made unto the house of Israel. . . .

Hearken, O ye Gentiles, and hear the words of Jesus Christ, the Son of the living God, which he hath commanded me that I should speak concerning you, for, behold he commandeth me that I should write, saying:

Turn, all ye Gentiles, from your wicked ways; and repent of your evil doings, of your lyings and deceivings, and of your whoredoms, and of your secret abominations, and your idolatries, and of your murders, and your priestcrafts, and your envyings, and your strifes, and from all your wickedness and abominations, and come unto me, and be baptized in my name, that ye may receive a remission of your sins, and be filled with the Holy Ghost, that ye may be numbered with my people who are of the house of Israel. (3 Nephi 29:5–9; 30:1–2)

The greatest legacy left to us by this great prophet was his own personal testimony of the Savior Jesus Christ. His whole life was a testimonial to the things he taught. Mormon himself was a living memorial to what he believed. Few in history could match the integrity of his purpose, the constancy of his commitment, and the endurance of his faith. To the last hour of his life, he was true to all he believed.

Now let us turn to Mormon's teachings on several subjects dear to his heart.

*chapter seven*

# FREEDOM AND EQUALITY

The twin subjects of freedom and equality are central to the doctrines of the Book of Mormon. Both spring from the God-given principle of agency. They are taught by all the Book of Mormon prophets. They were dear to Mormon, the man who fought throughout his life to preserve them. The foundational principle of agency, the freedom to choose, underlies the entire plan of salvation. It tells us the gate of heaven is open unto all who choose to enter and who will honor their covenant to follow Christ's teachings. "All men are privileged, the one like unto the other, and none are forbidden" (2 Nephi 26:28). Mormon includes his testimony of this vital principle:

> Thus we may see that the Lord is merciful unto all who will, in the sincerity of their hearts, call upon his holy name.
>
> Yea, thus we see that the gate of heaven is open unto all, even to those who will believe on the name of Jesus Christ, who is the Son of God. Yea, we see that whosoever will may lay hold upon the word of God, which is quick and powerful, which shall divide asunder all the cunning and the snares and the wiles of the devil, and lead the man of Christ in a strait and narrow course across that everlasting gulf of misery which is prepared to engulf the wicked—
>
> And land their souls, yea, their immortal souls, at the right hand of God in the kingdom of heaven, to sit down with Abraham, and Isaac, and with Jacob, and with all our holy fathers, to go no more out. (Helaman 3:27–30)

> Now I would that ye should understand that the word of God was
> liberal unto all, that none were deprived of the privilege of assembling
> themselves together to hear the word of God.
>
> Nevertheless the children of God were commanded that they
> should gather themselves together oft, and join in fasting and mighty
> prayer in behalf of the welfare of the souls of those who knew not
> God. (Alma 6:5–6)

The gate of heaven is open unto all. What a reassuring notion.

When Ammon, the son of King Mosiah, gained the favor of King
Lamoni and commenced preaching to the godless Lamanites, some
thought this a foolish adventure to an unworthy nation. But Mormon
draws our attention again to the underlying principle: The arm of the
Lord is extended to all who will repent. "And thus the work of the
Lord did commence among the Lamanites; thus the Lord did begin to
pour out his Spirit upon them; and we see that his arm is extended to
all people who will repent and believe on his name" (Alma 19:36).

Another aspect of agency is freedom of religion. This was at the
root of most of the troubles between the Nephites and the Lamanites.
The endless wars of Nephite history were fought to maintain it. Any
time wicked or willful men use unrighteous power to coerce free men
into bondage of any kind or to prevent them from worshiping God,
God is offended. There were always invading armies and apostates
within the ranks of the Nephites, ready to challenge this principle.
During the ninety years of the reign of the judges, one apostate after
another sought to lead the people of Christ away or to impose upon
them some form of bondage.

The infamous anti-Christ Korihor was one who, under the pre-
tense of liberating them from false doctrine, was instead leading his
followers into the captivity of Satan. In describing the work of this
villain, Mormon asserted the sacred principle that men are born to be
free. "Now there was no law against a man's belief; for it was strictly
contrary to the commands of God that there should be a law which
should bring men on to unequal grounds. For thus saith the scripture:
Choose ye this day, whom ye will serve. Now if a man desired to serve
God, it was his privilege; or rather, if he believed in God it was his
privilege to serve him; but if he did not believe in him there was no
law to punish him" (Alma 30:7–9).

How does freedom relate to war? This was a big question that troubled the Nephites as it has troubled men in all ages. What, if anything, justifies going to war? A troublesome question it is. Mormon's commentaries on the subject consistently defended the right of righteous people, when evil threatens their freedom, to defend their homes, their families, and their religion:

> Nevertheless, the Nephites were inspired by a better cause, for they were not fighting for monarchy nor power but they were fighting for their homes and their liberties, their wives and their children, and their all, yea, for their rites of worship and their church.
>
> They were doing that which they felt was the duty they owed to their God; for the Lord had said unto them, and also unto their fathers, that: Inasmuch as ye are not guilty of the first offense, neither the second, ye shall not suffer yourselves to be slain by the hands of your enemies.
>
> And again, the Lord has said that: Ye shall defend your families even unto bloodshed. Therefore for this cause were the Nephites contending with the Lamanites, to defend themselves, and their families, and their lands, their country, and their rights, and their religion. (Alma 43:45–47)

Mormon took the trouble to include an extreme example to illustrate the urgency of defending freedom; he recounted an incident in the life of the first Moroni. That famous captain, so honored by Mormon for his patriotism, not only rallied the country's patriots under the title of liberty, but he also moved with impressive initiative, exercising unusual powers of martial law to put down an insurrection aimed at destroying the liberty of his countrymen. Some would question the severity of his measures, even in an emergency and for a good cause. But Mormon apparently approved.

When large numbers of insurrectionists calling themselves Kingmen claimed superiority by virtue of their noble birth, and refused to take up arms, it seriously compromised the ability of Moroni's army to defend the country. The Book of Mormon describes Moroni as "exceedingly wroth" (Alma 51:14). He took decisive, immediate action, demonstrating that it was clearly unwise for an adversary to oppose the cause of freedom.

> And it came to pass that when Moroni saw this, and also saw that the Lamanites were coming into the borders of the land, he was exceedingly wroth because of the stubbornness of those people whom he had

labored with so much diligence to preserve; yea, he was exceedingly wroth; his soul was filled with anger against them.

And it came to pass that he sent a petition, with the voice of the people, unto the governor of the land, desiring that he should read it, and give him (Moroni) power to compel those dissenters to defend their country or to put them to death.

For it was his first care to put an end to such contentions and dissensions among the people; for behold, this had been hitherto a cause of all their destruction. And it came to pass that it was granted according to the voice of the people.

And it came to pass that Moroni commanded that his army should go against those king-men, to pull down their pride and their nobility and level them with the earth, or they should take up arms and support the cause of liberty.

And it came to pass that the armies did march forth against them; and they did pull down their pride and their nobility, insomuch that as they did lift their weapons of war to fight against the men of Moroni they were hewn down and leveled to the earth.

And it came to pass that there were four thousand of those dissenters who were hewn down by the sword; and those of their leaders who were not slain in battle were taken and cast into prison, for there was no time for their trials at this period.

And the remainder of those dissenters, rather than be smitten down to the earth by the sword, yielded to the standard of liberty, and were compelled to hoist the title of liberty upon their towers, and in their cities, and to take up arms in defence of their country.

And thus Moroni put an end to those king-men, that there were not any known by the appellation of king-men; and thus he put an end to the stubbornness and the pride of those people who professed the blood of nobility; but they were brought down to humble themselves like unto their brethren, and to fight valiantly for their freedom from bondage. (Alma 51:14–21)

*chapter eight*
# THE FRUITS OF RIGHTEOUSNESS

In the earliest pages of the Book of Mormon, Lehi taught his sons the relationship between righteousness and prosperity—prosperity both temporal and spiritual. This teaching, that a righteous life brings prosperity and rejecting Christ's teachings brings trouble, was repeated by King Benjamin, Alma, other Nephite prophets, and by Mormon. To highlight this principle, let's look at Lehi's words:

> Wherefore, I, Lehi, have obtained a promise, that inasmuch as those whom the Lord God shall bring out of the land of Jerusalem shall keep his commandments, they shall prosper upon the face of this land; and they shall be kept from all other nations, that they may possess this land unto themselves. And if it so be that they shall keep his commandments they shall be blessed upon the face of this land, and there shall be none to molest them, nor to take away the land of their inheritance; and they shall dwell safely forever.

> But behold, when the time cometh that they shall dwindle in unbelief, after they have received so great blessings from the hand of the Lord—having a knowledge of the creation of the earth, and all men, knowing the great and marvelous works of the Lord from the creation of the world; having power given them to do all things by faith; having all the commandments from the beginning, and having been brought by his infinite goodness into this precious land of promise—behold, I say, if the day shall come that they will reject the Holy One of Israel, the true Messiah, their Redeemer and their God, behold, the judgments of him that is just shall rest upon them. (2 Nephi 1:9–10)

As Mormon emphasized this true principle, he taught that humility leads to faith, faith leads to righteousness, and righteousness leads to God. "Nevertheless they did fast and pray oft, and did wax stronger and stronger in their humility, and firmer and firmer in the faith of Christ, unto the filling their souls with joy and consolation, yea, even to the purifying and the sanctification of their hearts, which sanctification cometh because of their yielding their hearts unto God" (Helaman 3:35).

Mormon pleaded with his people to repent, to humble themselves, and to remain steadfast in keeping the commandments. His own life was a great example, but he also pointed to the example of others who had been steadfast, like Captain Moroni, and described the fruits that followed the faithful. Moroni was "a man who was firm in the faith of Christ, and he had sworn with an oath to defend his people, his rights, and his country, and his religion, even to the loss of his blood" (Alma 48:13). The example of Moroni and his comrades-in-arms inspired his countrymen to righteousness. Their righteousness brought abundant peace and prosperity.

> And this was their faith, that by so doing God would prosper them in the land, or in other words, if they were faithful in keeping the commandments of God that he would prosper them in the land. . . .
>
> Now behold, Helaman and his brethren were no less serviceable unto the people than was Moroni; for they did preach the word of God, and they did baptize unto repentance all men whosoever would hearken unto their words.
>
> And thus they went forth, and the people did humble themselves because of their words, insomuch that they were highly favored of the Lord, and thus they were free from wars and contentions among themselves, yea, even for the space of four years. . . .
>
> Yea, and there was continual peace among them, and exceedingly great prosperity in the church because of their heed and diligence which they gave unto the word of God, which was declared unto them by Helaman, and Shiblon, and Corianton, and Ammon and his brethren, yea, and by all those who had been ordained by the holy order of God, being baptized unto repentance, and sent forth to preach among the people. (Alma 48:15, 19–20; 49:30)

> And they did prosper exceedingly, and they became exceedingly rich; yea, and they did multiply and wax strong in the land.

And thus we see how merciful and just are all the dealings of the Lord, to the fulfilling of all his words unto the children of men; yea, we can behold that his words are verified, even at this time, which he spake unto Lehi, saying: Blessed art thou and thy children; and they shall be blessed, inasmuch as they shall keep my commandments they shall prosper in the land. (Alma 50:18–20)

Here Mormon took care to insert a solemn warning:

But remember, inasmuch as they will not keep my commandments they shall be cut off from the presence of the Lord.

And we see that these promises have been verified to the people of Nephi; for it has been their quarrelings and their contentions, yea, their murderings, and their plunderings, their idolatry, their whoredoms, and their abominations, which were among themselves, which brought upon them their wars and their destructions.

And those who were faithful in keeping the commandments of the Lord were delivered at all times, whilst thousands of their wicked brethren have been consigned to bondage, or to perish by the sword, or to dwindle in unbelief, and mingle with the Lamanites.

But behold there never was a happier time among the people of Nephi, since the days of Nephi, than in the days of Moroni, yea, even at this time, in the twenty and first year of the reign of the judges. (Alma 50:20–23)

The above period of bliss was short lived. A great war resumed and continued for a long period of time. But finally, as the war came to a close, we see again the happy state that follows a return to righteousness:

But behold, because of the exceedingly great length of the war between the Nephites and the Lamanites many had become hardened . . . and many were softened because of their afflictions, insomuch that they did humble themselves before God, even in the depth of humility . . . and there was once more peace established among the people of Nephi. . . .

Therefore, Helaman and his brethren went forth, and did declare the word of God with much power unto the convincing of many people of their wickedness, which did cause them to repent of their sins and to be baptized unto the Lord their God. . . .

And the people of Nephi began to prosper again in the land, and began to multiply and to wax exceedingly strong again in the land. And they began to grow exceedingly rich.

> But notwithstanding their riches, or their strength, or their pros-
> perity, they were not lifted up in the pride of their eyes; neither were
> they slow to remember the Lord their God; but they did humble
> themselves exceedingly before him.
>
> Yea, they did remember how great things the Lord had done for
> them, that he had delivered them from death, and from bonds, and
> from prisons, and from all manner of afflictions, and he had delivered
> them out of the hands of their enemies.
>
> And they did pray unto the Lord their God continually, insomuch
> that the Lord did bless them, according to his word, so that they did
> wax strong and prosper in the land. (Alma 62:41–42, 45, 48–51)

The story of the conversion of the Lamanite nation to the Lord's
gospel is a missionary story unprecedented in the world's history. This
massive conversion of a heathen people was initiated by the four sons of
King Mosiah. The four sons themselves were first converted—deeply
converted—from their own wickedness. Then, at great peril to their
own lives, they went into Lamanite country and became the Lord's
instruments in bringing thousands of souls unto Christ. The results of
their mission were spectacular.

> And thousands were brought to the knowledge of the Lord, yea,
> thousands were brought to believe in the traditions of the Nephites;
> and they were taught the records and prophecies which were handed
> down even to the present time.
>
> And as sure as the Lord liveth, so sure as many as believed, or as
> many as were brought to the knowledge of the truth, through the
> preaching of Ammon and his brethren, according to the spirit of rev-
> elation and of prophecy, and the power of God working miracles in
> them—yea, I say unto you, as the Lord liveth, as many of the Laman-
> ites as believed in their preaching, and were converted unto the Lord,
> never did fall away.
>
> For they became a righteous people; they did lay down the weap-
> ons of their rebellion, that they did not fight against God any more,
> neither against any of their brethren. (Alma 23:5–7)

> And thus we see that, when these Lamanites were brought to
> believe and to know the truth, they were firm, and would suffer even
> unto death rather than commit sin; and thus we see that they buried
> their weapons of peace, or they buried the weapons of war, for peace.
> (Alma 24:19)

> And [the people of Ammon] were . . . numbered among the people who were of the church of God. And they were also distinguished for their zeal towards God, and also towards men; for they were perfectly honest and upright in all things; and they were firm in the faith of Christ, even unto the end.
>
> And they did look upon shedding the blood of their brethren with the greatest abhorrence; and they never could be prevailed upon to take up arms against their brethren; and they never did look upon death with any degree of terror, for their hope and views of Christ and the resurrection; therefore, death was swallowed up to them by the victory of Christ over it. . . .
>
> And thus they were a zealous and beloved people, a highly favored people of the Lord. (Alma 27:27–28, 30)

A popular and inspiring story from this era is about the two thousand stripling warriors, who "had been taught by their mothers that if they did not doubt, God would deliver them" (Alma 56:47). This story strikingly illustrates the truth that a righteous life brings great blessings. These stripling warriors were the children of Lamanites who had been converted by Ammon and his brethren and who had made an unbreakable covenant that they would never again take up arms. But now, in the face of a mortal threat from invading Lamanites, they were troubled over being a heavy burden upon their Nephite brethren. They were troubled over being helpless to defend themselves. They came close to breaking their oath and joining in the war but were persuaded otherwise by Helaman, "lest by so doing they should lose their souls" (Alma 53:15).

> But behold, it came to pass they had many sons, who had not entered into a covenant that they would not take their weapons of war to defend themselves against their enemies; therefore they did assemble themselves together at this time, as many as were able to take up arms, and they called themselves Nephites.
>
> And they entered into a covenant to fight for the liberty of the Nephites, yea, to protect the land unto the laying down of their lives; yea, even they covenanted that they never would give up their liberty, but they would fight in all cases to protect the Nephites and themselves from bondage.
>
> Now behold, there were two thousand of those young men, who entered into this covenant and took their weapons of war to defend their country.

And now behold, as they never had hitherto been a disadvantage to the Nephites, they became now at this period of time also a great support; for they took their weapons of war, and they would that Helaman should be their leader.

And they were all young men, and they were exceedingly valiant for courage, and also for strength and activity; but behold, this was not all—they were men who were true at all times in whatsoever thing they were entrusted.

Yea, they were men of truth and soberness, for they had been taught to keep the commandments of God and to walk uprightly before him. (Alma 53:16–21)

Now they never had fought, yet they did not fear death; and they did think more upon the liberty of their fathers than they did upon their lives; yea, they had been taught by their mothers, that if they did not doubt, God would deliver them. . . .

And it came to pass that the Lamanites took courage and began to pursue them . . . when Helaman came upon their rear with his two thousand, and began to slay them exceedingly, insomuch that the whole army of the Lamanites halted and turned upon Helaman. . . .

And now it came to pass that we, the people of Nephi, the people of Antipus, and I with my two thousand, did surround the Lamanites, and did slay them. . . .

And now it came to pass that when they had surrendered themselves up unto us, behold, I numbered those young men who had fought with me, fearing lest there were many of them slain.

But behold, to my great joy, there had not one soul of them fallen to the earth; yea, and they had fought as if with the strength of God; yea, never were men known to have fought with such miraculous strength; and with such mighty power did they fall upon the Lamanites, that they did frighten them; and for this cause did the Lamanites deliver themselves up as prisoners of war. (Alma 56:47, 52, 54–56) *chapter nine*

# BEWARE OF PRIDE

Why is it that people richly favored of the Lord, prospering in righteousness, happy and fulfilled, cannot cope with the blessings that they receive? Why would anyone reject the promises made to the faithful and choose instead a lifestyle that brings misery?

Why did Mormon's people so resolutely pursue the course leading to destruction? Over and over, Mormon mourned this phenomenon. He pointed to the fate of those who, once enlightened, had turned to sin. He devoted a whole chapter (Helaman 12) to discussing this vexing trait of human nature—mankind's tendency to deliberately choose evil over good. "O how foolish, and how vain, and how evil, and devilish, and how quick to do iniquity, and how slow to do good, are the children of men" (Helaman 12:4). In our own day, we too ask ourselves why men persist in the tendency to choose the Prince of Darkness over the Prince of Peace.

> And it came to pass that all these iniquities did come unto them in the space of not many years. . . .
>
> And they did grow in their iniquities . . . to the great sorrow and lamentation of the righteous.
>
> And thus we see that the Nephites did begin to dwindle in unbelief, and grow in wickedness and abominations, while the Lamanites began to grow exceedingly in the knowledge of their God; yea, they did begin to keep his statutes and commandments, and to walk in truth and uprightness before him.
>
> And thus we see that the Spirit of the Lord began to withdraw

from the Nephites, because of the wickedness and the hardness of their hearts.

And thus we see that the Lord began to pour out his Spirit upon the Lamanites, because of their easiness and willingness to believe in his words. (Helaman 6:32–36)

And thus we can behold how false, and also the unsteadiness of the hearts of the children of men; yea, we can see that the Lord in his great infinite goodness doth bless and prosper those who put their trust in him.

Yea, and we may see at the very time when he doth prosper his people, yea, in the increase of their fields, their flocks and their herds, and in gold, and in silver, and in all manner of precious things of every kind and art; sparing their lives, and delivering them out of the hands of their enemies; softening the hearts of their enemies that they should not declare wars against them; yea, and in fine, doing all things for the welfare and happiness of his people; yea, then is the time that they do harden their hearts, and do forget the Lord their God, and do trample under their feet the Holy One—yea, and this because of their ease, and their exceedingly great prosperity.

And thus we see that except the Lord doth chasten his people with many afflictions, yea, except he doth visit them with death and with terror, and with famine and with all manner of pestilence, they will not remember him. . . .

Yea, how quick to be lifted up in pride; yea, how quick to boast, and do all manner of that which is iniquity; and how slow are they to remember the Lord their God, and to give ear unto his counsels, yea, how slow to walk in wisdom's paths!

Behold, they do not desire that the Lord their God, who hath created them, should rule and reign over them; notwithstanding his great goodness and his mercy towards them, they do set at naught his counsels, and they will not that he should be their guide.

O how great is the nothingness of the children of men; yea, even they are less than the dust of the earth.

For behold, the dust of the earth moveth hither and thither, to the dividing asunder, at the command of our great and everlasting God. . . .

Therefore, blessed are they who will repent and hearken unto the voice of the Lord their God; for these are they that shall be saved.

And may God grant, in his great fulness, that men might be brought unto repentance and good works, that they might be restored unto grace for grace, according to their works.

And I would that all men might be saved. (Helaman 12:1–3, 5–8; 23–25)

Mormon identified two root causes of most of the troubles of the Nephites: pride and satan. These two evil influences have threatened mankind throughout history. The first of these troublemakers was pride, which grows out of the willful and perverse nature of human beings. Ultimately, according to Mormon, pride was a main cause of the destruction of the Nephite nation. "Behold, the pride of this nation, or the people of the Nephites, hath proven their destruction except they should repent" (Moroni 8:27).

Throughout the Book of Mormon, this perversity of human nature is highlighted by Mormon. Both the Nephite and Lamanite nations repeatedly rejected the formula for happiness taught by the prophets. The Lamanites were notoriously hardhearted. In the beginning, Laman and Lemuel knew the truth. They had seen an angel and the power of God made manifest, but they rejected this knowledge and would not live by the truth. In the pride of their hearts they deliberately taught their children ways of wickedness and rebellion, and without the guidance of the Spirit of God their posterity dwindled in unbelief.

When the missionary sons of Mosiah went southward to preach among the Lamanites, they found them wholly without the enlightenment of the Spirit of God.

> [They were] a wild and a hardened and a ferocious people; a people who delighted in murdering the Nephites, and robbing and plundering them; and their hearts were set upon riches, or upon gold and silver, and precious stones; yet they sought to obtain these things by murdering and plundering, that they might not labor for them with their own hands.
>
> Thus they were a very indolent people, many of whom did worship idols, and the curse of God had fallen upon them because of the traditions of their fathers; notwithstanding the promises of the Lord were extended unto them on the conditions of repentance. (Alma 17:14–15)

On the other hand, the Nephites had benefited from the teachings of righteous prophets. When they had heeded these teachings, they had prospered. But even though great leaders taught them truth, too often the haughtiness of pride entered in.

As he chronicled the times of Helaman I and II, Mormon dwelt at length on the misfortunes that followed pride. The following recital in Mormon's words is a classic case study of this insidious vice in its many manifestations. When Helaman II was serving as chief judge, a period of unusual prosperity occurred. But then the monster entered the scene.

> And it came to pass that in this same year there was exceedingly great prosperity in the church, insomuch that there were thousands who did join themselves unto the church and were baptized unto repentance.
>
> And so great was the prosperity of the church, and so many the blessings which were poured out upon the people, that even the high priests and the teachers were themselves astonished beyond measure.
>
> And it came to pass that the work of the Lord did prosper unto the baptizing and uniting to the church of God, many souls, yea even tens of thousands. . . .
>
> And in the fifty and first year of the reign of the judges there was peace also, save it were the pride which began to enter into the church. . . .
>
> [The people] were lifted up in pride, even to the persecution of many of their brethren. Now this was a great evil, which did cause the more humble part of the people to suffer great persecutions, and to wade through much affliction . . . [because of] the exceedingly great pride which had gotten into the hearts of the people; and it was because of their exceedingly great riches and their prosperity in the land; and it did grow upon them from day to day. (Helaman 3:24–26, 33–34, 36)

Following on the heels of pride came "many dissensions" and much contention. Then "much bloodshed" by fellow citizens and brethren. The narrative follows the march of evil through the land, noting the inevitable bitter harvest, as Mormon documents this cause of so much sorrow:

> Now this great loss of the Nephites, and the great slaughter which was among them, would not have happened had it not been for their wickedness and their abomination which was among them; yea, and it was among those also who professed to belong to the church of God.
>
> And it was because of the pride of their hearts, because of their exceeding riches, yea, it was because of their oppression to the poor, withholding their food from the hungry, withholding their clothing from the naked, and smiting their humble brethren upon the cheek,

making a mock of that which was sacred, denying the spirit of prophecy and of revelation, murdering, plundering, lying, stealing, committing adultery, rising up in great contentions. . . .

And because of this their great wickedness, and their boastings in their own strength, they were left in their own strength; therefore they did not prosper, but were afflicted and smitten, and driven before the Lamanites, until they had lost possession of almost all their lands. . . .

They had altered and trampled under their feet the laws of Mosiah, or that which the Lord commanded him to give unto the people; and they saw that their laws had become corrupted, and that they had become a wicked people, insomuch that they were wicked even like unto the Lamanites.

And because of their iniquity the church had begun to dwindle; and they began to disbelieve in the spirit of prophecy and in the spirit of revelation; and the judgments of God did stare them in the face.

And they saw that they had become weak, like unto their brethren, the Lamanites, and that the Spirit of the Lord did no more preserve them; yea, it had withdrawn from them because the Spirit of the Lord doth not dwell in unholy temples—

Therefore the Lord did cease to preserve them by his miraculous and matchless power, for they had fallen into a state of unbelief and awful wickedness. . . .

And thus had they fallen into this great transgression; yea, thus had they become weak, because of their transgression, in the space of not many years. (Helaman 4:11–13, 22–26)

Another manifestation of trouble in this ancient land was the recurring corruption within the government. This was spawned by the perverse nature of the people, whose pride led them to reject Christ's teachings and to follow the teachings of Satan. An ominous change in their affairs occurred when these people, who had lived under a democratic government, began deliberately to choose evil rather than good. Mormon had read Mosiah's warning about this long before. Mosiah had warned them to watch out when the voices of free people deliberately choose evil. He wrote:

Now it is not common that the voice of the people desireth anything contrary to that which is right; but it is common for the lesser part of the people to desire that which is not right; therefore this shall ye observe and make it your law—to do your business by the voice of the people.

> And if the time comes that the voice of the people doth choose iniquity, then is the time that the judgments of God will come upon you; yea, then is the time he will visit you with great destruction even as he has hitherto visited this land. (Mosiah 29:26–27)

As Mormon read about this time in history, he observed it happening again in his own society. Brief interludes of peace seemed always to be followed by unrighteousness. Here is one example from the time of Helaman II: "Their laws and their governments were established by the voice of the people, and they who chose evil were more numerous than they who chose good, therefore they were ripening for destruction, for the laws had become corrupted. Yea, and this was not all; they were a stiffnecked people, insomuch that they could not be governed by the law nor justice, save it were to their destruction" (Helaman 5:2–3).

Another example stands out in Mormon's account of the time following the glorious era recorded in 4 Nephi, as the Saints gradually lost their way and headed for disaster:

> They did not dwindle in unbelief, but they did wilfully rebel against the gospel of Christ; and they did teach their children that they should not believe. . . .
>
> And they did still continue to build up churches unto themselves, and adorn them with all manner of precious things. . . .
>
> And it came to pass that the wicked part of the people began again to build up the secret oaths and combinations of Gadianton.
>
> And also the people who were called the people of Nephi began to be proud in their hearts, because of their exceeding riches, and become vain like unto their brethren, the Lamanites.
>
> And from this time the disciples began to sorrow for the sins of the world. (4 Nephi 1:38, 41–44)

Ultimately, "wickedness did prevail upon the face of the whole land, insomuch that the Lord did take away his beloved disciples, and the work of miracles and of healing did cease because of the iniquity of the people. And there were no gifts from the Lord, and the Holy Ghost did not come upon any, because of their wickedness and unbelief" (Mormon 1:13–14).

# chapter ten

# BEWARE OF THE EVIL ONE

In addition to pride, which was the product of the willful and perverse nature of the people, the other root cause of the downfall of the Nephite nation was the destructive work of Satan. Of course, Satan, in a general sense, is the cause of all evil. But I speak here of situations involving the welfare of nations, groups, and individuals, when Satan wages war in vicious and specific ways. With millennia of experience behind him, he has learned of areas of weakness in mankind, which he can exploit with impressive efficiency. He has discovered ways to bring down both individuals and kingdoms, and he pursues his mission with great effectiveness.

To accomplish his designs, Satan works through ambitious or willing subjects, and persuades them they are doing something worthwhile. One classic case was Korihor, whose sophistry and "great swelling words" (Alma 30:31) caused great mischief. Korihor's confession, when it finally came, identified Satan (in the unlikely role of an angel) as the sponsor of his apostasy:

> But behold, the devil hath deceived me; for he appeared unto me in the form of an angel, and said unto me: Go and reclaim this people, for they have all gone astray after an unknown God. And he said unto me: There is no God; yea, and he taught me that which I should say. And I have taught his words; and I have taught them because they were pleasing unto the carnal mind; and I taught them, even until I had much success, insomuch that I verily believed that they were true; and for this cause I withstood the truth, even until I have brought this great curse upon me. (Alma 30:53)

The story of Korihor (see Alma 30) has personal application in each of our lives as we consider the devious and cunning ways of Lucifer, that evil one. He is real and he is dangerous!

In the end, Satan will not support his followers. After recording Alma's account of the rise and fall of Korihor, Mormon concluded with a good lesson about what happens when people follow Satan in an attempt to subvert the truth. After being exposed, cast out, and reduced to begging food for his support, Korihor was "run upon and trodden down; even until he was dead. And thus we see the end of him who perverteth the ways of the Lord; and thus we see that the devil will not support his children at the last day, but doth speedily drag them down to hell" (Alma 30:59–60).

That Satan will abandon his followers seems obvious enough as we read it. But it is not obvious to some. Mormon marveled at what he saw in apostates from the Church. Once they abandoned the Holy Ghost, who reveals and testifies of truth, they could no longer distinguish between truth and error. No longer did they even recognize truth. Not only did they apostatize, but when they did so, they seemed often to become the most vile of sinners and the most dangerous of enemies.

> And thus we can plainly discern, that after a people have been once enlightened by the Spirit of God, and have had great knowledge of things pertaining to righteousness, and then have fallen away into sin and transgression, they become more hardened, and thus their state becomes worse than though they had never known these things. (Alma 24:30)

> Now these dissenters, having the same instruction and the same information of the Nephites, yea, having been instructed in the same knowledge of the Lord, nevertheless, it is strange to relate, not long after their dissensions they became more hardened and impenitent, and more wild, wicked and ferocious than the Lamanites—drinking in with the traditions of the Lamanites; giving way to indolence, and all manner of lasciviousness; yea, entirely forgetting the Lord their God. (Alma 47:36)

One wicked dissenter written of by Helaman was the notorious Amalickiah, who wanted to be king of the Nephites. When he could not prevail against Moroni and his title of liberty, he led many away in rebellion and eventually became a king of the Lamanites. Mormon drew another lesson from the mischief caused by this rascal: One very bad person can cause much trouble for many others.

> And there were many in the church who believed in the flattering words of Amalickiah, therefore they dissented even from the church; and thus were the affairs of the people of Nephi exceedingly precarious and dangerous, notwithstanding their great victory which they had had over the Lamanites, and their great rejoicings which they had had because of their deliverance by the hand of the Lord.
>
> Thus we see how quick the children of men do forget the Lord their God, yea, how quick to do iniquity, and to be led away by the evil one.
>
> Yea, and we also see the great wickedness one very wicked man can cause to take place among the children of men.
>
> Yea, we see that Amalickiah, because he was a man of cunning device and a man of many flattering words, that he led away the hearts of many people to do wickedly; yea, and to seek to destroy the church of God, and to destroy the foundation of liberty which God had granted unto them, or which blessing God had sent upon the face of the land for the righteous' sake. (Alma 46:7–10)

## Secret Combinations

The true work of God goes forth in broad daylight, where everyone can see and hear. Satan's work is often shrouded in secrecy. Satan chose the ancient curse of secret combinations to work his will upon the Nephites. Mormon identified Gadianton as the founding father of the secret societies that brought such ruin to the nation. About fifty years before the birth of Christ, an evil man named Kishkumen appeared and soon won a disciple—Gadianton. Mormon explains, "[Kishkumen] was upheld by his band, who had entered into a covenant that no one should know his wickedness. [And] there was one Gadianton, who was exceedingly expert in many words, and also in his craft, to carry on the secret work of murder and of robbery; therefore he became the leader of the band of Kishkumen. . . . And behold, in the end of this book ye shall see that this Gadianton did prove the overthrow, yea almost the entire destruction of the people of Nephi" (Helaman 2:3–4, 13).

The phrase "exceedingly expert in many words" became descriptive of many leaders of secret societies in the Book of Mormon. We see it today in faithless leaders in our own country.

We also see among the Gadiantons the corrupted use of the word *covenant*, which properly denotes a commitment by the people to obey their God. This word also has legal implications, meaning "a contract." Kishkumen's evil band prostituted the word and entered into unholy covenants with one another and with Satan. Satan's followers have used covenants ever since Cain slew his brother Abel. Pay close attention; the following description of evil covenants is a classic outline of the devious methods of Lucifer.

> Satan did stir up the hearts of the more part of the Nephites, insomuch that they did unite with those bands of robbers, and did enter into their covenants and their oaths, that they would protect and preserve one another in whatsoever difficult circumstances they should be placed, that they should not suffer for their murders, and their plunderings, and their stealings.
>
> And it came to pass that they did have their signs, yea, their secret signs, and their secret words; and this that they might distinguish a brother who had entered into the covenant, that whatsoever wickedness his brother should do he should not be injured by his brother, nor by those who did belong to his band, who had taken this covenant.
>
> And thus they might murder, and plunder, and steal, and commit whoredoms and all manner of wickedness, contrary to the laws of their country and also the laws of their God.
>
> And whosoever of those who belonged to their band should reveal unto the world of their wickedness and their abominations, should be tried, not according to the laws of their country, but according to the laws of their wickedness, which had been given by Gadianton and Kishkumen . . .
>
> Now behold, these secret oaths and covenants . . . were put into the heart of Gadianton by that same being who did entice our first parents to partake of the forbidden fruit—
>
> Yea, that same being who did plot with Cain, that if he would murder his brother Abel it should not be known unto the world. And he did plot with Cain and his followers from that time forth.
>
> And also it is that same being who . . . spread the works of darkness and abominations over all the face of the land, until he dragged the people down to an entire destruction, and to an everlasting hell.
>
> Yea, it is that same being who put it into the heart of Gadianton to still carry on the work of darkness, and of secret murder; and he has brought it forth from the beginning of man even down to this time.

And behold, it is he who is the author of all sin. And behold, he doth carry on his works of darkness and secret murder, and doth hand down their plots, and their oaths, and their covenants, and their plans of awful wickedness, from generation to generation according as he can get hold upon the hearts of the children of men. (Helaman 6:21–24, 26–30)

The work of the secret combinations often included the use of "flattering words," so often cited in the scriptures. But these evil men also knew where power was found. At every opportunity, they infiltrated government and the legal system. In this movement, corrupt lawyers were the prominent leaders. A little more than twenty years before the birth of the Savior, the Nephite people were again engulfed in wickedness. The government was controlled by corrupt lawyers bound together under their evil covenants.

[Nephi,] seeing the people in a state of such awful wickedness, and those Gadianton robbers filling the judgment-seats—having usurped the power and authority of the land; laying aside the commandments of God, and not in the least aright before him; doing no justice unto the children of men;

Condemning the righteous because of their righteousness; letting the guilty and the wicked go unpunished because of their money; and moreover to be held in office at the head of government, to rule and do according to their wills, that they might get gain and glory of the world, and, moreover, that they might the more easily commit adultery, and steal, and kill, and do according to their own wills. . . .

He did exclaim in the agony of his soul: Oh, that I could have had my days in the days when my father Nephi first came out of the land of Jerusalem, that I could have joyed with him in the promised land; then were his people easy to be entreated, firm to keep the commandments of God, and slow to be led to do iniquity; and they were quick to hearken unto the words of the Lord. (Helaman 7:4–7)

Not long after this episode, Satan was exploiting the weakness of pride in the people to the point that they were knowingly and willfully rebelling against their God. Mormon repeatedly mentioned this state of understanding the commandments and then choosing to disobey. It finally brought down the ultimate judgment of God—the wholesale destruction of the wicked at the time of the Crucifixion.

Some were lifted up in pride [because of their exceedingly great riches], and others were exceedingly humble; some did return railing for railing, while others would receive railing and persecution and all manner of afflictions, and would not turn and revile again, but were humble and penitent before God. . . .

Now the cause of this iniquity of the people was this—Satan had great power, unto the stirring up of the people to do all manner of iniquity, and to the puffing them up with pride, tempting them to seek for power, and authority, and riches, and the vain things of the world.

And thus Satan did lead away the hearts of the people to do all manner of iniquity. . . .

Now they did not sin ignorantly, for they knew the will of God concerning them; therefore they did willfully rebel against God. (3 Nephi 6:13, 15–16, 18)

> And all this iniquity had come upon the people because they did yield themselves unto the power of Satan.
>
> And the regulations of the government were destroyed, because of the secret combination of the friends and kindreds of those who murdered the prophets. (3 Nephi 7:5–6)

Mormon's description of the root causes of trouble in the world is a graphic warning to those who will hearken. It is one of the great contributions of Mormon and of the Book of Mormon. If we pay attention, we can identify and avoid the work of Satan, the great deceiver.

*chapter eleven*

# Basic Christian Virtues

What did Mormon say about the simple, basic Christian virtues? Consider the circumstances of his life. Almost from the moment of his birth, Mormon was immersed in an evil culture. He must have had very few good examples among his boyhood friends. Most of his associates through life were men of war, with instincts much different from his. He was a general of armies. His profession was war. His job was to destroy wicked Lamanites, and he was very good at it—he must have been or he would never have survived. He was surrounded all his life by wicked Nephites—vile and bloodthirsty, constantly seeking revenge and destruction. Mormon's life was dependent upon destroying his enemies before they destroyed him. He was occupied with surviving the constant threat of hatred, violence, and annihilation.

It required a great heart and a noble spirit to rise above all this and to spend one's best efforts in preaching about the great Christian virtues. Mormon had such a heart and spirit. Few have demonstrated such an uncompromised love for mankind as did Mormon, or a greater desire for the welfare of others.

Mormon, this man of war, was a good man clear to the core. His deepest instincts and his greatest hopes were for the welfare of his fellow men. His very nature defined him as a man of God. From his writings we learn of the ideals that lay closest to his heart: equality, charity, sacrifice, thankfulness, patience, faith in Christ. These are but a few of the values taught in the Book of Mormon—values that were highlighted in the words of this man of many virtues.

### Equality of all mankind and charity for the needy

These two ideals are near the top of Mormon's list. He wrote:

> The preacher was no better than the hearer, neither was the teacher any better than the learner; and thus they were all equal, and they did all labor, every man according to his strength.
>
> And they did impart of their substance, every man according to that which he had, to the poor, and the needy, and the sick, and the afflicted; and they did not wear costly apparel, yet they were neat and comely. . . .
>
> And now, because of the steadiness of the church they began to be exceedingly rich, having abundance of all things whatsoever they stood in need—an abundance of flocks and herds, and fatlings of every kind, and also abundance of grain, and of gold, and of silver, and of precious things, and abundance of silk and fine-twined linen, and all manner of good homely cloth.
>
> And thus, in their prosperous circumstances, they did not send away any who were naked, or that were hungry, or that were athirst, or that were sick, or that had not been nourished; and they did not set their hearts upon riches; therefore they were liberal to all, both old and young, both bond and free, both male and female, whether out of the church or in the church, having no respect to persons as to those who stood in need. (Alma 1:26–27, 29–30)

### Sacrifice for others

Over time, many great men appeared on the ancient American scene. Their lives of sacrifice were chronicled by Mormon. Among the noblest of these were the sons of King Mosiah. After their conversion, each of these gave up the right to succeed his father as king. They turned away from the opportunity for fame and fortune and worldly pursuits in favor of a mission fraught with great peril, abuse, imprisonment, and almost every other hardship. The dedicated and miraculous missionary work of these men brought many to Christ. Their lives of sacrifice brought hope and the joy of righteousness to thousands who otherwise would have been doomed during their lives to the unhappiness that follows wickedness.

> Now they were desirous that salvation should be declared to every creature, for they could not bear that any human soul should perish; yea, even the very thoughts that any soul should endure endless torment did cause them to quake and tremble.

And thus did the Spirit of the Lord work upon them, for they were the very vilest of sinners. And the Lord saw fit in his infinite mercy to spare them; nevertheless they suffered much anguish of soul because of their iniquities, suffering much and fearing that they should be cast off forever. (Mosiah 28:3–4)

A wonderful testimonial to the rewards of their sacrifice for others is found in the ecstatic recitation by Ammon of the sufferings he and his brothers endured for the cause. Mormon must have smiled as he read of these stalwart disciples who, like himself, discovered that there really is no such thing as sacrifice for the Savior. Even extreme sacrifices can, in the end, be counted as blessings. In his service we seem always to come out ahead.

And we have suffered every privation . . . and we have been cast out, and mocked, and spit upon, and smote upon our cheeks; and we have been stoned, and taken and bound with strong cords, and cast into prison; and through the power of God we have been delivered again.

And we have suffered all manner of afflictions, and all this, that perhaps we might be the means of saving some soul. . . .

Now have we not reason to rejoice? Yea, I say unto you, there never were men that had so great reason to rejoice as we, since the world began. (Alma 26:28–30, 35)

## Thankfulness

The Lord is pleased to provide bounteous blessings when the receiver acknowledges his goodness with a grateful heart. He is disappointed when the real source of blessings is overlooked. Often in prosperity, the Nephites, no more than some of their latter-day counterparts, were slow to humble themselves in appreciation. The people of Limhi had become careless, faithless, and sinful, and had suffered terribly under Lamanite oppressors. But they were teachable.

And they did humble themselves even in the depths of humility; and they did cry mightily to God; yea, even all the day long did they cry unto their God that he would deliver them out of their afflictions.

And now the Lord was slow to hear their cry because of their iniquities; nevertheless the Lord did hear their cries, and began to soften the hearts of the Lamanites that they began to ease their burdens; yet the Lord did not see fit to deliver them out of bondage.

And it came to pass that they began to prosper by degrees in the land, and began to raise grain more abundantly, and flocks, and herds, that they did not suffer with hunger. (Mosiah 21:14–16)

Mormon highlighted the thankful reaction of another community of Nephites who had been spared in a great battle:

And they did rejoice and cry again with one voice, saying: May the God of Abraham, and the God of Isaac, and the God of Jacob, protect this people in righteousness, so long as they shall call on the name of their God for protection.

And it came to pass that they did break forth, all as one, in singing, and praising their God for the great thing which he had done for them, in preserving them from falling into the hands of their enemies.

Yea, they did cry: Hosanna to the Most High God. And they did cry: Blessed be the name of the Lord God Almighty, the Most High God.

And their hearts were swollen with joy, unto the gushing out of many tears, because of the great goodness of God in delivering them out of the hands of their enemies; and they knew it was because of their repentance and their humility that they had been delivered from an everlasting destruction. (3 Nephi 4:30–33)

When the protracted war in the time of Captain Moroni had concluded, peace and prosperity returned. Mormon quickly pointed out the dramatic difference made by the change from war to peace. And he praised their attitude of thanksgiving.

And the people of Nephi began to prosper again in the land, and began to multiply and to wax exceedingly strong again in the land. And they began to grow exceedingly rich.

But notwithstanding their riches, or their strength, or their prosperity, they were not lifted up in the pride of their eyes; neither were they slow to remember the Lord their God; but they did humble themselves exceedingly before him.

Yea, they did remember how great things the Lord had done for them, that he had delivered them from death, and from bonds, and from prisons, and from all manner of afflictions and he had delivered them out of the hands of their enemies.

And they did pray unto the Lord their God continually, insomuch that the Lord did bless them, according to his word, so that they did wax strong and prosper in the land. (Alma 62:48–51)

### Patience in affliction

The Lord does not always remove our burdens, but he will always help us deal with them. When fleeing from the Waters of Mormon, Alma's people lodged temporarily in the land of Helam. Here they lived righteously, even while under the oppressive rule of a cruel tribe of Lamanites, and began to prosper. But much of the fruits of their labors was paid in tribute to their oppressors.

> And it came to pass that the voice of the Lord came to them in their afflictions, saying: Lift up your heads and be of good comfort, for I know of the covenant which ye have made unto me; and I will covenant with my people and deliver them out of bondage.
>
> And I will also ease the burdens which are put upon your shoulders, that even you cannot feel them upon your backs, even while you are in bondage; and this will I do that ye may stand as witnesses for me hereafter, and that ye may know of a surety that I, the Lord God, do visit my people in their afflictions.
>
> And now it came to pass that the burdens which were laid upon Alma and his brethren were made light; yea, the Lord did strengthen them that they could bear up their burdens with ease, and they did submit cheerfully and with patience to all the will of the Lord.
>
> And it came to pass that so great was their faith and their patience that the voice of the Lord came unto them again, saying: Be of good comfort, for on the morrow I will deliver you out of bondage. . . .
>
> And Alma and his people departed into the wilderness; and when they had traveled all day they pitched their tents in a valley. . . .
>
> Yea, and in the valley of Alma they poured out their thanks to God because he had been merciful unto them, and eased their burdens, and had delivered them out of bondage; for they were in bondage, and none could deliver them except it were the Lord their God.
>
> And they gave thanks to God, yea, all their men and all their women and all their children that could speak lifted their voices in the praises of their God. (Mosiah 24:13–16, 20–22)

### No contention

Little practiced in the world, rarely fully appreciated, but a virtue with profound implications for society, the importance of avoiding contention is a major lesson in the Book of Mormon. This matter loomed large in Mormon's long life and was a haunting factor in his final days.

Several hundred years earlier, when the Savior had first appeared to the Nephites, in his very first sermon to them and in the most simple terms, he had defined his doctrine: Men must repent and be baptized and become as little children. And, emphatically, the Savior had commanded, "Verily, verily I say unto you, he that hath the spirit of contention is not of me, but is of the devil, who is the father of contention, and he stirreth up the hearts of men to contend with anger, one with another. Behold, this is not my doctrine, to stir up the hearts of men with anger, one against another; but this is my doctrine, that such things should be done away" (3 Nephi 11:29–30).

Mormon, this warrior/prophet, was engulfed throughout his life in the most bitter contention among men. By the end, he'd had enough of it! As he sat down to write the few verses describing the blissful state in 4 Nephi, it would be fair to suppose that his mind was on the bitter warfare that swirled around him. Contention ruled the day. This devilish state of affairs must have occupied his mind. Possibly without even realizing it, Mormon repeated four times in a few verses, "There was no contention."

> And there were no contentions and disputations among them. . . .
>
> And it came to pass that there was no contention among all the people, in all the land. . . .
>
> And it came to pass that there was no contention in the land, because of the love of God which did dwell in the hearts of the people. . . .
>
> For the Lord did bless them in all their doings . . . and there was no contention in all the land. (4 Nephi 1:2, 13, 15, 18)

Let this serve as a worthy lesson among the many taught by Mormon, the great man of war who became an apostle of peace. Let it be taught in our churches, in our homes, and in our families. Let it be practiced in our communities. Let it be remembered that contention is of the devil, who is the father of contention. The Savior said, "This is my doctrine, that such things should be done away" (3 Nephi 11:30).

### Faith in Christ, the supreme virtue

Mormon wrote with admiration for the third Nephi, grandson of Helaman II and son of another noble prophet named Nephi. This Nephi had labored for his people without ceasing in preparation for the Savior and was on hand to greet Christ when he appeared in the New World following his crucifixion. He became the leader of the

Twelve Apostles on the American continent (3 Nephi 19:4, 11–12). That Nephi was a valiant soul, that his heart was pure, and that his faith produced miracles, was attested by Mormon:

> And it came to pass that Nephi—having been visited by angels and also the voice of the Lord, therefore having seen angels, and being eye-witness, and having had power given unto him that he might know concerning the ministry of Christ, and also being eye-witness to their quick return from righteousness unto their wickedness and abominations;
>
> Therefore, being grieved for the hardness of their hearts and the blindness of their minds—went forth among them in that same year, and began to testify, boldly, repentance and remission of sins through faith on the Lord Jesus Christ. . . . And Nephi did minister with power and with great authority.
>
> So great was his faith on the Lord Jesus Christ that angels did minister unto him daily.
>
> And in the name of Jesus did he cast out devils and unclean spirits; and even his brother did he raise from the dead, after he had been stoned and suffered death by the people. (3 Nephi 7:15–19)

There are three more virtues we will discuss more fully in the next chapter—faith; hope; and charity, and the pure love of Christ. In his own life Mormon practiced them all.

*chapter twelve*

# FAITH, HOPE, AND CHARITY

Moroni, Mormon's valiant son, finished his father's work on the plates and then hid up the records to be brought forth in a future day. Before finishing, he added a few chapters of his own, including a brief abridgement of the history of the people of Jared and Jared's brother, who had come many centuries before from the Tower of Babel. As Moroni concludes his record, it is as though he says to us, "This cannot be complete without including a great sermon my father gave and a letter he once sent to me. These contain inspiring doctrine. But they also will provide a tribute to my noble father. These will put a finishing touch on the work of this man's life, and the spirit with which he performed his work."

Chapters 7 and 8 of Moroni are the words of Mormon himself. These words speak for themselves and could serve as an epitaph to his life. We do not know when they were written, but it was probably toward the end of his life. It does not matter; his views and feelings did not change, and his words reveal his constant, compassionate heart. They are a memorial to the ideals that motivated him.

Sometime before his final battles, Mormon wrote to his "beloved son, Moroni." He prayed for him and invoked the goodness and grace of God upon him. He raised the banner of Christ, who called only sinners to repentance. Mormon appealed for understanding of the truth that little children are not sinners but are alive in Christ. We must become like little children, must love them with a perfect love and apply the mercy of Christ unto them. This wonderful message about the baptism of little children is not only about baptism. It is about faith, hope, and charity.

My beloved son, Moroni, I rejoice exceedingly that your Lord Jesus Christ hath been mindful of you, and hath called you to his ministry, and to his holy work.

I am mindful of you always in my prayers, continually praying unto God the Father in the name of his Holy Child, Jesus, that he, through his infinite goodness and grace, will keep you through the endurance of faith on his name to the end. . . .

Listen to the words of Christ, your Redeemer, your Lord and your God. Behold, I came into the world not to call the righteous but sinners to repentance; the whole need no physician, but they that are sick; wherefore, little children are whole, for they are not capable of committing sin; wherefore the curse of Adam is taken from them in me, that it hath no power over them; and the law of circumcision is done away in me. . . .

Behold I say unto you that this thing shall ye teach—repentance and baptism unto those who are accountable and capable of committing sin; yea, teach parents that they must repent and be baptized, and humble themselves as their little children, and they shall all be saved with their little children. . . .

But little children are alive in Christ, even from the foundation of the world; if not so, God is a partial God, and also a changeable God, and a respecter to persons; for how many little children have died without baptism! . . .

Behold I say unto you, that he that supposeth that little children need baptism is in the gall of bitterness and in the bonds of iniquity; for he hath neither faith, hope, nor charity; wherefore, should he be cut off while in the thought, he must go down to hell. . . .

And I am filled with charity, which is everlasting love; wherefore, all children are alike unto me; wherefore, I love little children with a perfect love; and they are all alike and partakers of salvation.

For I know that God is not a partial God, neither a changeable being; but he is unchangeable from all eternity to all eternity.

Little children cannot repent; wherefore, it is awful wickedness to deny the pure mercies of God unto them, for they are all alive in him because of his mercy. . . .

Behold, my son, I will write unto you again if I go not out soon against the Lamanites. Behold, the pride of this nation, or the people of the Nephites, hath proven their destruction except they should repent.

Pray for them, my son, that repentance may come unto them. But behold, I fear lest the Spirit hath ceased striving with them; and in this part of the land they are also seeking to put down all power and authority which cometh from God; and they are denying the Holy Ghost. . . .

Farewell, my son, until I shall write unto you, or shall meet you again. Amen. (Moroni 8:2–30)

As his life drew near to its close, this man had every reason to be disenchanted, disappointed, bitter, and cynical. Almost everything he had labored for in life failed in the end. The ideals he cherished, the people he loved, the causes he gave his life for—all were gone. Gone too was his whole family, except for one son. The Lamanites had killed his father and mother, his brothers and sisters, his people (see Mormon 8:3, 5). They had annihilated his civilization.

Yet, out of the deepest sorrow of his heart, his last recorded words were of mercy, love, charity—and a final call to repentance. What other general of defeated armies, what other lonely survivor of holocaust, would speak with sincere love about these "brethren," would plead with the Lord for their welfare in the last days, would prophesy great blessings upon them?

There seem to be only two likely explanations for this paradox. First, Mormon was a thoroughly Christian man and believed with his whole soul all that he taught. Every Christian teaching he espoused spoke of hope, lifted the spirit, and pointed one to heaven. Mormon lived in a bitter world but was not bitter. He was in this world but was not confined to this world. He was of a higher caliber. His whole soul, his very nature, responded to the call of the Savior, "Come unto me."

The second explanation for Mormon's unconquerable Christian spirit is that his greatest preoccupation was his message for the future. Though he wrote about the past, he did not dwell in the past. His mind did not dwell even in the present. His vision was of the future, his thoughts were of the future, and his best life's work was for the future. As a prophet, he had almost no followers in his own day. He was a prophet to future generations whom he saw only in vision. These were his people—we were his people. In a very real sense, Mormon is our own prophet—a prophet of the latter days.

Mormon had been exposed to Christ's sermons on faith, hope, and charity. He, like the apostle Paul—and using some of the same words—

taught eloquently this supreme doctrine, which was not his own but the Savior's. These words are granite monuments to true Christianity and are foundations for all other virtues.

Mormon's discourse on the three virtues is found in Moroni chapter 7. He begins with a plea for good works, for prayer with real intent. In these verses Mormon teaches the sources of good and evil: "All things which are good cometh of God; and that which is evil cometh of the devil." It's that simple. And the way to judge between good and evil is equally simple, if one understands the above rule. The light within us gives us all the means to discern truth.

Then follows Mormon's explanation of charity and of its precursors: faith and hope. Some would argue that it is contradictory to speak of faith and hope as dependent upon each other. Are they not at two ends of the spectrum, one a proclamation of strength, the other a sign of weakness? No, says Mormon, and he explains why we cannot have one without the other. When we have faith in Christ, and faith in the truth of his great doctrines of salvation, we can then hope for all good things. We can hope for a brighter day, for the welfare of our families, for life with God in the hereafter.

Faith and hope together beget charity, the crowning virtue, the pure love of Christ. May we all be filled with this love at the close of our lives, as was Mormon at the end of his. Read thoughtfully and ponder carefully his words.

> I would speak unto you that are of the church, that are the peaceable followers of Christ, and that have obtained a sufficient hope by which ye can enter into the rest of the Lord, from this time henceforth until ye shall rest with him in heaven. . . .
>
> For I remember the word of God which saith by their works ye shall know them; for if their works be good, then they are good also.
>
> For behold, God hath said a man being evil cannot do that which is good; for if he offereth a gift, or prayeth unto God, except he shall do it with real intent it profiteth him nothing. . . .
>
> For behold, if a man being evil giveth a gift, he doeth it grudgingly; wherefore it is counted unto him the same as if he had retained the gift; wherefore he is counted evil before God.
>
> And likewise also is it counted evil unto a man, if he shall pray and not with real intent of heart; yea, and it profiteth him nothing, for God receiveth none such. . . .
>
> Wherefore, all things which are good cometh of God; and that

which is evil cometh of the devil; for the devil is an enemy unto God, and fighteth against him continually, and inviteth and enticeth to sin, and to do that which is evil continually.

But behold, that which is of God inviteth and enticeth to do good continually; wherefore, every thing which inviteth and enticeth to do good, and to love God, and to serve him, is inspired of God.

Wherefore, take heed, my beloved brethren, that ye do not judge that which is evil to be of God, or that which is good and of God to be of the devil. . . .

For behold, the Spirit of Christ is given to every man, that he may know good from evil; wherefore, I show unto you the way to judge; for every thing which inviteth to do good, and to persuade to believe in Christ, is sent forth by the power and gift of Christ; wherefore ye may know with a perfect knowledge it is of God.

But whatsoever thing persuadeth men to do evil, and believe not in Christ, and deny him, and serve not God, then ye may know with a perfect knowledge it is of the devil; for after this manner doth the devil work, for he persuadeth no man to do good, no, not one; neither do his angels; neither do they who subject themselves unto him. . . .

And after that he came men also were saved by faith in his name; and by faith, they become the sons of God. And as surely as Christ liveth he spake these words unto our fathers, saying: Whatsoever thing ye shall ask the Father in my name, which is good, in faith believing that ye shall receive, behold, it shall be done unto you . . .

And Christ hath said: If ye will have faith in me ye shall have power to do whatsoever thing is expedient in me.

And he hath said: Repent all ye ends of the earth, and come unto me, and be baptized in my name, and have faith in me, that ye may be saved. . . . For no man can be saved, according to the words of Christ, save they shall have faith in his name; wherefore, if these things have ceased, then has faith ceased also; and awful is the state of man, for they are as though there had been no redemption made. . . .

And again, my beloved brethren, I would speak unto you concerning hope. How is it that ye can attain unto faith, save ye shall have hope?

And what is it that ye shall hope for? Behold I say unto you that ye shall have hope through the atonement of Christ and the power of his resurrection, to be raised unto life eternal, and this because of your faith in him according to the promise.

Wherefore, if a man have faith he must needs have hope; for without faith there cannot be any hope. . . .

[A man] must needs have charity. And charity suffereth long, and is kind, and envieth not, and is not puffed up, seeketh not her own, is not easily provoked, thinketh no evil, and rejoiceth not in iniquity but rejoiceth in the truth, beareth all things, believeth all things, hopeth all things, endureth all things.

Wherefore, my beloved brethren, if ye have not charity, ye are nothing, for charity never faileth. Wherefore, cleave unto charity, which is the greatest of all, for all things must fail—

But charity is the pure love of Christ, and it endureth forever; and whoso is found possessed of it at the last day, it shall be well with him.

Wherefore, my beloved brethren, pray unto the Father with all the energy of heart, that ye may be filled with this love, which he hath bestowed upon all who are true followers of his Son, Jesus Christ; that ye may become the sons of God; that when he shall appear we shall be like him, for we shall see him as he is; that we may have this hope; that we may be purified even as he is pure. Amen. (Moroni 7:3–48) *chapter thirteen*

# REPENT AND COME UNTO CHRIST

Hearken! At the close of his account in 3 Nephi, which describes the Savior's ministry in the New World, Mormon repeated his call to mankind to hearken to the words of Christ. To hearken means more than just to listen. It means to take heed, to actively follow, and to repent. Mormon is pleading with readers to avoid the trouble that follows those who refuse to hearken.

> Wo be unto him that will not hearken unto the words of Jesus, and also to them whom he hath chosen and sent among them; for whoso receiveth not the words of Jesus and the words of those whom he hath sent receiveth not him; and therefore he will not receive them at the last day. (3 Nephi 28:34)
>
> And now behold, I say unto you that when the Lord shall see fit, in his wisdom, that these sayings shall come unto the Gentiles according to his word, then ye may know that the covenant which the Father hath made with the children of Israel . . . is already beginning to be fulfilled.
>
> And ye may know that the words of the Lord, which have been spoken by the holy prophets, shall all be fulfilled. . . .
>
> And ye need not imagine in your hearts that the words which have been spoken are vain, for behold, the Lord will remember his covenant which he hath made unto his people of the house of Israel.
>
> And when ye shall see these sayings coming forth among you, then ye need not any longer spurn at the doings of the Lord, for the sword of his justice is in his right hand; and behold, at that day, if ye shall spurn at his doings he will cause that it shall soon overtake you.

Wo unto him that spurneth at the doings of the Lord; yea, wo unto him that shall deny the Christ and his works! (3 Nephi 29:1–5)

Repent! In the messages of all the prophets through the ages, the most recurrent theme is repentance. We are urgently counseled to keep the commandments and to flee from Satan—but when we falter or fail, we are urged to repent quickly.

As mortals on this earth, each one of us is at risk. As sons and daughters of our Eternal Father, each may succeed in eternity's greatest adventure. But each, too, may fail. With divine daring, God our Father has placed his beloved children on earth in a situation in which they are exposed to life-threatening evil and are subject to eternal death—spiritual death. Our Father knows the risks we face, and he chooses to take these risks because his purpose for us requires it. In order for us to succeed in the huge enterprise of everlasting life, he has allowed exposure to the possibility of everlasting failure.

If we succeed in this supernal adventure, we gain everything. Even if we fail, in his mercy he provides for us a kingdom of lesser glory. Only if we despise him and completely reject him are we lost forever from his everlasting family.

Repent! This is the theme of the prophets. This is the theme of Mormon, and he has shown us the way. In every discourse or commentary, the warning to repent is found, either expressed or implied. Though he despaired of failure with his stubborn contemporaries, he never ceased to call upon them to mend their ways and return to their faith in Christ. His earliest desire, even at age fifteen, was to call his people to repentance. His last lament was over the slain of his people who had refused to repent, who had "rejected that Jesus, who stood with open arms to receive [them]" (Mormon 6:17).

He wrote, "O that ye had repented before this great destruction had come upon you. But behold, ye are gone, and the Father, yea, the Eternal Father of heaven, knoweth your state; and he doeth with you according to his justice and mercy" (Mormon 6:22).

Mormon's own people rejected his pleadings. What of us, of the latter days? How could he impress us sufficiently to help us escape a repetition of history? Repent, and come unto Christ! As with all the other prophets, Mormon's warnings were followed by an invitation.

And now behold, I, Mormon, do not desire to harrow up the souls of men in casting before them such an awful scene of blood and carnage as was laid before mine eyes; but . . . that a knowledge of these things must come unto the remnant of these people, and also unto the Gentiles . . . I write a small abridgement. . . .

And this is the commandment which I have received . . . that [the unbelieving] may be persuaded that Jesus is the Christ, the Son of the living God; that the Father may bring about, through his most Beloved, his great and eternal purpose, in restoring the Jews, or all the house of Israel, to the land of their inheritance, which the Lord their God hath given them, unto the fulfilling of his covenant;

And also that the seed of this people may more fully believe his gospel, which shall go forth unto them from the Gentiles; for this people shall be scattered, and shall become a dark, a filthy, and a loathsome people, beyond the description of that which ever hath been amongst us, yea, even that which hath been among the Lamanites, and this because of their unbelief and idolatry.

For behold, the Spirit of the Lord hath already ceased to strive with their fathers; and they are without Christ and God in the world; and they are driven about as chaff before the wind.

They were once a delightsome people, and they had Christ for their shepherd; yea, they were led even by God the Father.

But now, behold, they are led about by Satan, even as chaff is driven before the wind, or as a vessel is tossed about upon the waves, without sail or anchor, or without anything wherewith to steer her; and even as she is, so are they. (Mormon 5:8–9, 13–18)

Know ye that ye must come unto repentance, or ye cannot be saved.

Know ye that ye must lay down your weapons of war, and delight no more in the shedding of blood, and take them not again, save it be that God shall command you.

Know ye that ye must come to the knowledge of your fathers, and repent of all your sins and iniquities, and believe in Jesus Christ, that he is the Son of God, and that he was slain by the Jews, and by the power of the Father he hath risen again, whereby he hath gained the victory over the grave; and also in him is the sting of death swallowed up.

Therefore repent, and be baptized in the name of Jesus, and lay hold upon the gospel of Christ. (Mormon 7:3–5, 8)

### The doctrine of Christ

Christ's doctrine is found throughout the scriptures. Yet the simplicity of his doctrine is nowhere more plainly stated than in the account written on the plates of the Book of Mormon. According to Mormon, when the Savior appeared to the Nephites following his crucifixion, he first identified himself and proved his identity with the wounds from the cross. Then he instructed his disciples about baptism. And then, in that first glorious appearance, he declared repeatedly his simple and wonderful doctrine. His words must surely have pleased Mormon, his plain-spoken prophet:

> Behold, verily, verily, I say unto you, I will declare unto you my doctrine.
>
> And this is my doctrine, which the Father hath given unto me . . . whoso believeth in me, and is baptized, the same shall be saved; and they are they who shall inherit the kingdom of God.
>
> And whoso believeth not in me, and is not baptized, shall be damned.
>
> Verily, verily, I say unto you, that this is my doctrine. . . .
>
> And again I say unto you, ye must repent, and become as a little child, and be baptized in my name, or ye can in no wise receive these things. . . .
>
> Verily, verily, I say unto you, that this is my doctrine. (3 Nephi 11:31–35, 37, 39)

Mormon embraced this doctrine and taught it. Throughout his life in the world of wicked men, he retained his love for the simple virtues of little children: "I love little children with a perfect love; and they are all alike and partakers of salvation. . . . For behold that all little children are alive in Christ" (Moroni 8:17, 22).

During the 170 years following the ministry of the Savior among his "other sheep," a condition of righteousness and supreme happiness had been achieved. These people were supremely happy, not because they had discovered the tree of life but because they lived the gospel of Jesus Christ almost perfectly. Their way of living brought happiness. It brought paradise to earth.

It is curious that so little is said by Mormon, or by any other prophet, about this period of time. Readers are led to wonder if the more complete record of these people might be part of the sealed portion of the Book of Mormon. Perhaps in this nearly-exalted Nephite society there were happenings and communion about which we are not yet worthy to hear.

For whatever reason, we have only two pages of commentary summarizing this entire period of time. Still, as we read Mormon's brief synopsis of 4 Nephi, we see the message repeated loud and clear: Obedience to the Law of God brings happiness. That it brings happiness in the hereafter, most everyone would agree—that is an easy doctrine. But could we dare to hope that a fullness of joy—complete happiness—could be achieved here, in this disorderly world? The record of 4 Nephi answers, yes, it has happened before! The key to this secret garden is obedience to God's law.

As we now conclude, let us read from the postscript to the Savior's life. Those amazing 170 years of bliss that followed Christ's ministry on earth describe the Savior's message of hope for a better world:

> And there were no contentions and disputations among them, and every man did deal justly one with another.
>
> And they had all things common among them; therefore there were not rich and poor, bond and free, but they were all made free, and partakers of the heavenly gift. . . . And there still continued to be peace in the land.
>
> And there were great and marvelous works wrought by the disciples of Jesus, insomuch that they did heal the sick, and raise the dead, and cause the lame to walk, and the blind to receive their sight, and the deaf to hear; and all manner of miracles did they work among the children of men; and in nothing did they work miracles save it were in the name of Jesus. . . .
>
> And the Lord did prosper them exceedingly in the land . . . And now, behold, it came to pass that the people of Nephi did wax strong, and did multiply exceedingly fast, and became an exceedingly fair and delightsome people. . . .
>
> They did walk after the commandments which they had received from their Lord and their God, continuing in fasting and prayer, and in meeting together oft both to pray and to hear the word of the Lord.
>
> And it came to pass that there was no contention among all the people, in all the land; but there were mighty miracles wrought among the disciples of Jesus. . . .
>
> And it came to pass that there was no contention in the land, because of the love of God which did dwell in the hearts of the people.

And there were no envyings, nor strifes, nor tumults, nor whoredoms, nor lyings, nor murders, nor any manner of lasciviousness; and surely there could not be a happier people among all the people who had been created by the hand of God.

There were no robbers, nor murderers, neither were there Lamanites, nor any manner of -ites; but they were in one, the children of Christ, and heirs to the kingdom of God.

And how blessed were they! For the Lord did bless them in all their doings; yea, even they were blessed and prospered until an hundred and ten years had passed away; and the first generation from Christ had passed away, and there was no contention in all the land. (4 Nephi 1:2–18)

At the beginning of this book, we invited Mormon's faithful son, Moroni, to introduce us to the work of his father. We quoted the words of Moroni from Mormon chapter 8 and from the title page of the Book of Mormon. In his own words, Moroni graphically describes the latter days—our own day!—in which the Book of Mormon would be brought "out of darkness unto light . . . by the power of God" (Mormon 8:16). It would come in a day when the blood of the Saints would cry unto the Lord, when churches and their leaders would be corrupted, and when natural and manmade disasters would abound; in a day when great pollutions and abominations of all kinds would lead the people astray.

As we close, let us turn again to Moroni for his parting exhortation, which concludes with the most important of all the admonitions from both himself and his father—come unto Christ. Many of his day heard Mormon's message and did not heed it. But there was one—his son, Moroni—who did.

From out of the dust of his ancient, solitary, amazing vantage point in history, faithful Moroni, the one surviving son of mighty Mormon, left his own stirring challenge to us of the latter days. Fifteen hundred years later, this same Moroni, then a glorified, resurrected being (see the introduction to the Book of Mormon), appeared to the young prophet Joseph Smith and delivered Mormon's book to the waiting world.

And again I would exhort you that ye would come unto Christ, and lay hold upon every good gift, and touch not the evil gift, nor the unclean thing.

And awake, and arise from the dust, O Jerusalem; yea, and put on thy beautiful garments, O daughter of Zion; and strengthen thy stakes and enlarge thy borders forever, that thou mayest no more be confounded, that the covenants of the Eternal Father which he hath made unto thee, O house of Israel, may be fulfilled.

Yea, come unto Christ, and be perfected in him, and deny yourselves of all ungodliness; and if ye shall deny yourselves of all ungodliness, and love God with all your might, mind and strength, then is his grace sufficient for you, that by his grace ye may be perfect in Christ. (Moroni 10:30–32)

# About the Author

Angus Belliston's understanding and appreciation of the Book of Mormon has come simply from reading it and hearing it taught over a lifetime. His hope in writing is to share some insights about the prophet Mormon that will add to our appreciation for this great man and for the book he helped bring to us—the Book of Mormon.

Mr. Belliston is a retired banker and has served the Church as a teacher, bishop, stake president, regional representative, mission president, and as a counselor in temple presidencies. He and his wife, Jenny, reside in Provo, Utah. They are the parents of eleven, the grandparents of thirty-nine, and the great-grandparents of eleven.